zine scene

by

Francesca Lia Block

&

Hillary Carlip

Designed by Hillary Carlip

Published by GIRL PRESS

ISBN #09659754-3-6
First Edition
13579108642
Library of Congress CIP Number: 98-88173
Cover artwork and illustration on title page by Anthony Freda
Design production by Amy Inouye

Dedicated to

our moms

Mim Carlip

and

Gilda Block

and to the creative spirits of our fathers

Bob and Irving

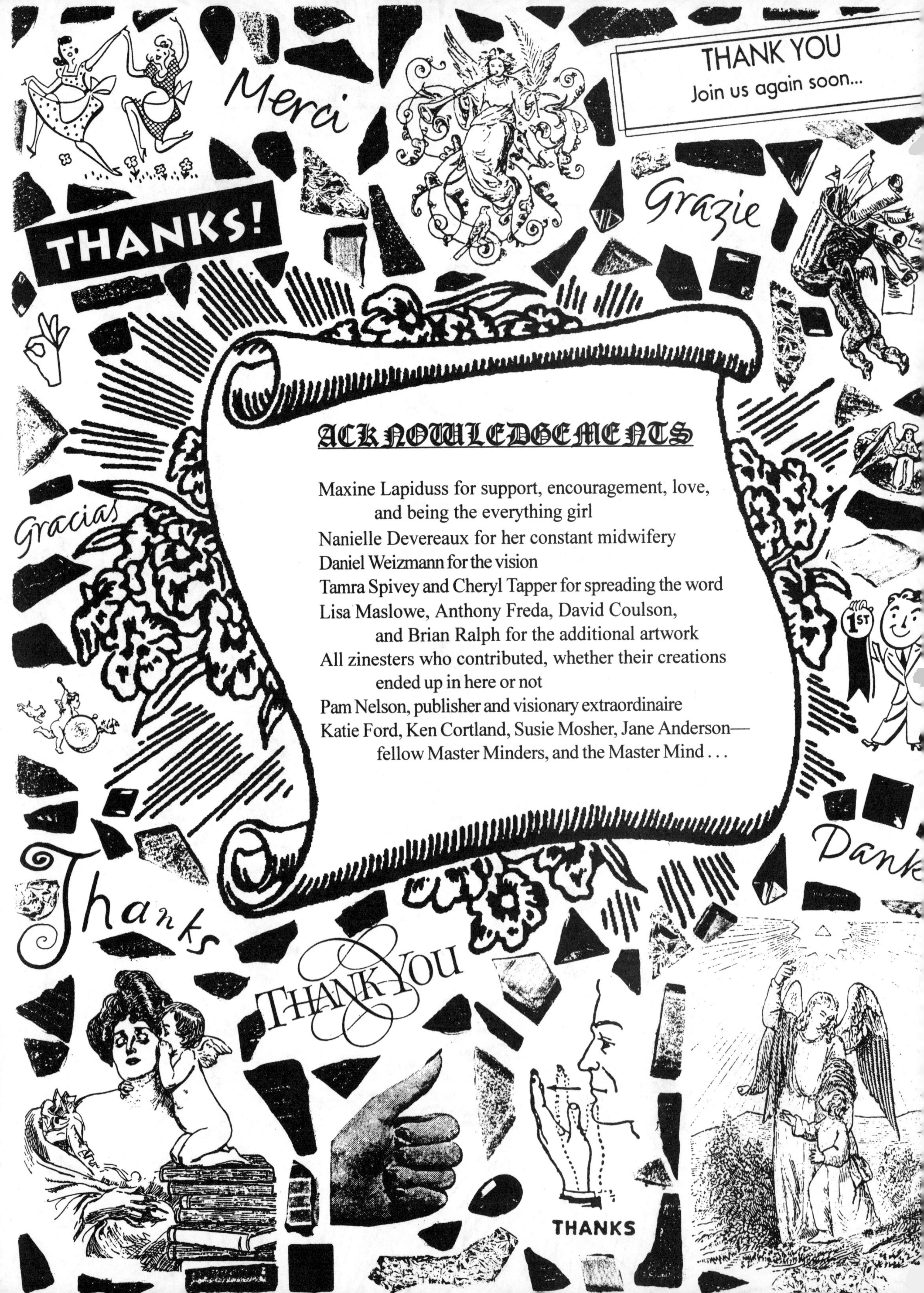

ACKNOWLEDGEMENTS

Maxine Lapiduss for support, encouragement, love, and being the everything girl

Nanielle Devereaux for her constant midwifery

Daniel Weizmann for the vision

Tamra Spivey and Cheryl Tapper for spreading the word

Lisa Maslowe, Anthony Freda, David Coulson, and Brian Ralph for the additional artwork

All zinesters who contributed, whether their creations ended up in here or not

Pam Nelson, publisher and visionary extraordinaire

Katie Ford, Ken Cortland, Susie Mosher, Jane Anderson—fellow Master Minders, and the Master Mind . . .

TABLE OF CONTENTS

SECTION THREE: GETTING YOUR ZINE SEEN

INTRO

"... Yay for the zine. Power tool for me. My drill, my jackhammer to make noise with. I'll give it a hug and a tug and sleep with it. I'll steal a heart with it (if only I knew how). I'll hate it and wish I'd never printed it, I'll love it when others tell me they love it, I'll blush when it falls into the wrong hands and I'll cry when I read it next year. ..."

- Michelle Morgan Cross, age 14
ADVERSARIA and SMUDGE zines

People of every age, race, gender, economic standing, sexual preference, and belief system are writing, designing, printing, and selling their own zines—hand-made publications that combine elements of personal journals, newsletters, and magazines. They're cutting, pasting, scribbling, scrawling, etching, sketching, collaging, collating, stapling, taping, licking, sticking, addressing, stamping, trading, collecting, concocting, feeling, healing, brewing, renewing. Anyone can join in, even if they don't have the privilege of being able to read and write, because zines can also be compiled of images, or even made from found objects. This D.I.Y. (Do It Yourself) aspect is what makes zines so revolutionary. It might seem contradictory to be reading a how-to guide for something that is DIY, but we hope ZINE SCENE will encourage you to do it your way.

Tell your story ...

your obsessions

your fears

your dreams

in words and pics

because it is powerful

because it kicks

to express and connect

even if it's not always pretty, cool, or slick.

So, if you're ready to make your own zine, or if you've already been zine-ing for years but would like to know what other zinesters are up to; if you need some ideas about design or distribution, or if you'd like to learn about computer e-zines, then come with us. Let's go to Zineland!

Discover the Miracle

Millions agree:
"The most exciting
discovery in years

it's a
secret...
(but soon it will be on everybody's lips)

Looking for Something?

Are you in the know?

Can this be true

Special Offer!
to introduce you

PLEASE TELL M

Between us...

It's a
Red
Letter
Day!

You don't believe it at first.

MAKING Light OF IT

SECTION ONE
ZINE GREEN?
ALL YOU NEED TO KNOW ABOUT ZINES

A WHAT?

WHAT IT IZZZZZ

Zines come in all shapes and sizes. Some are just a page or two, others much longer. They can be photocopied or finely printed, done on the backs of discarded office papers or on pricey card stock, handwritten with collages or designed on a computer using different fonts. They can be purchased for anywhere from ten cents to ten dollars; some are free, or just the cost of a stamp.

What's inside is even more varied. Some have specific focuses: Per-zines (personal writings); Sfanzines (sci-fi); Music zines; Girl zines; Queer Zines; Comix, Spiritual, Political, Literary zines, and more. They can be about anything. See for yourself:

BANANA LABEL TIMES (FOR NANA-STICKER COLLECTORS)

BIG PAIN (childhood trauma)

CAN CONTROL (photos of graffiti)

DAVKA—*Jewish Cultural Revolution*

DREAMWORLD NEWS (DREAMS AS NEWS STORIES)

THE E TICKET—COLLECTING THEME PARK MEMORIES

ERASER CARVER'S QUARTERLY (eraser carving as an art form)

FAT!SO?—*For people who don't apologize for their size*

4 LETTER WORD—*Rape*

FUNK 'N' GROOVE ('70S CULTURE)

GEEKGIRL; GEEKCORE; RIOT NERD (celebrating dorkiness)

HERBAL VOICES—THE JOURNAL OF SELF-RELIANT HERBALISM

HIPMAMA—THE PARENTING ZINE

HIP HOP HOUSEWIFE—*FOR HOMEMAKERS WITH ATTITUDE*

I HATE YOU—*Love Stories from Hell*

MAC AND ME (Macaulay Culkin obsession)

NATION (PEN PAL LETTERS)

PEZ COLLECTOR'S NEWS (CANDY DISPENSER JOURNAL)

POODLE (bowling and poodles)

SAINTS PRESERVE US (hagiography, feast days, charts, etc.)

SNACKS (reproductions of missing pet posters)

TIKI NEWS (tiki/exotica culture, memorabilia, music)

FLYPAPER (band flyers)

QUIET DESPERATION (found objects)

VINYL WOK (recipes from indie rock stars)

WE LIKE POO (a scatological study)

Here are a few samples from specific types of zines:

COMIX

Comix can be quietly personal like 29-year-old Jeff Guarino's THE RUMBLING UNDERNEATH (in which he explores themes such as death, sex, and chocolate chip cookies) . . .

1930
THE WORLD STOPPED MAKING SENSE IN 1917
THAT'S WHAT GRANDPA SAID TO ME AT GRANDMA'S FUNERAL
WHILE WE ATE PUMPKIN PIE EVEN THOUGH IT WASN'T
CHRISTMAS
I DIDN'T KNOW WHAT HE MEANT AT THE TIME BUT
I THOUGHT HE WAS PROBABLY RIGHT...
AND LOOK AT HER HERE -- ALL LEGS AND AMORPHOUS
SHADOWS
AND LOOK AT HIM THERE -- THE STRENGTH IN HIS STANCE
AND THEY LOOK NOTHING LIKE I REMEMBER THEM.

FIVE YEARS LATER, SITTING ON HIS LONELY
LOP-SIDED SOFA
I ASKED GRANDPA WHY HE'D SAID WHAT HE'D SAID THAT DAY
AND HE TOLD ME HE COULDN'T REMEMBER BUT HE DID SAY
IT SOUNDED LIKE A PIECE OF WISDOM.
THEN HE TOLD ME TO GO GET HIM A WALNUT FROM
THAT BOWL OVER THERE
AND WHEN I CAME BACK TO HIM HIS EYES WERE
CLOSED
BUT I THINK HE WAS FAKING...
MAYBE HE WAS THINKING OF DEAD FRIENDS AND
BOWLING TROPHIES.

TWO YEARS LATER HE REMARRIED BUT I WASN'T
INVITED TO THE CEREMONY
NO ONE WAS
HE'D ELOPED WITH HIS SIXTY-FOUR YEAR OLD BRIDE TO
LAS VEGAS FOR WHAT HE LATER CALLED
THE BEST KIND OF WEDDING
THE KIND WITH NO RELATIVES...
AND I WONDER IF HIS THOUGHTS WANDERED BACK AT ALL
TO HIS PAST WITH GRANDMA.

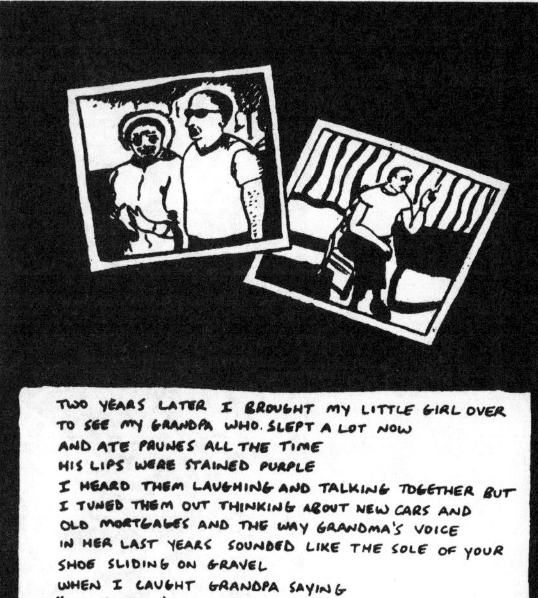
TWO YEARS LATER I BROUGHT MY LITTLE GIRL OVER
TO SEE MY GRANDPA WHO SLEPT A LOT NOW
AND ATE PRUNES ALL THE TIME
HIS LIPS WERE STAINED PURPLE
I HEARD THEM LAUGHING AND TALKING TOGETHER BUT
I TUNED THEM OUT THINKING ABOUT NEW CARS AND
OLD MORTGAGES AND THE WAY GRANDMA'S VOICE
IN HER LAST YEARS SOUNDED LIKE THE SOLE OF YOUR
SHOE SLIDING ON GRAVEL
WHEN I CAUGHT GRANDPA SAYING
"...AND THAT'S WHY THE WORLD JUST DON'T MAKE SENSE
NOT SINCE 1917, ANYWAY."
I TURNED IN TIME TO SEE A STRANGE GLIMMER OF
UNDERSTANDING IN MY DAUGHTER'S EYES AS SHE NODDED
SMILING AT THE OLD MAN.

excerpts from piece in THE RUMBLING UNDERNEATH #2

. . . or they can be more in-yr-face like 23-year-old Brian Ralph's FIREBALL pieces.

excerpts from FIREBALL #4 & 5

The main thing with comix is to let the pics rock, roll, and moan louder than wor

MUSIC ZINES

Music is one of the subjects that many people feel most passionate about. Maybe that's because, as an art form, it can affect you physically, emotionally, and spiritually all at once.

Zines, in fact, were born out of the punk rock music scene in the '70s. They were originally referred to as Fanzines, because they usually focused on bands and performers. Although fanzines today such as REALLY DEEP THOUGHTS (Tori Amos), SIN FANZINE (Nine Inch Nails), KISSAHOLICS (The Kiss Kollector Zine), and B-HIVE (B 52's) may have one focus, there are a lot of music zines that feature a wide variety of artists and music. David Smay's PALE BLUE LOUIE is one of them.

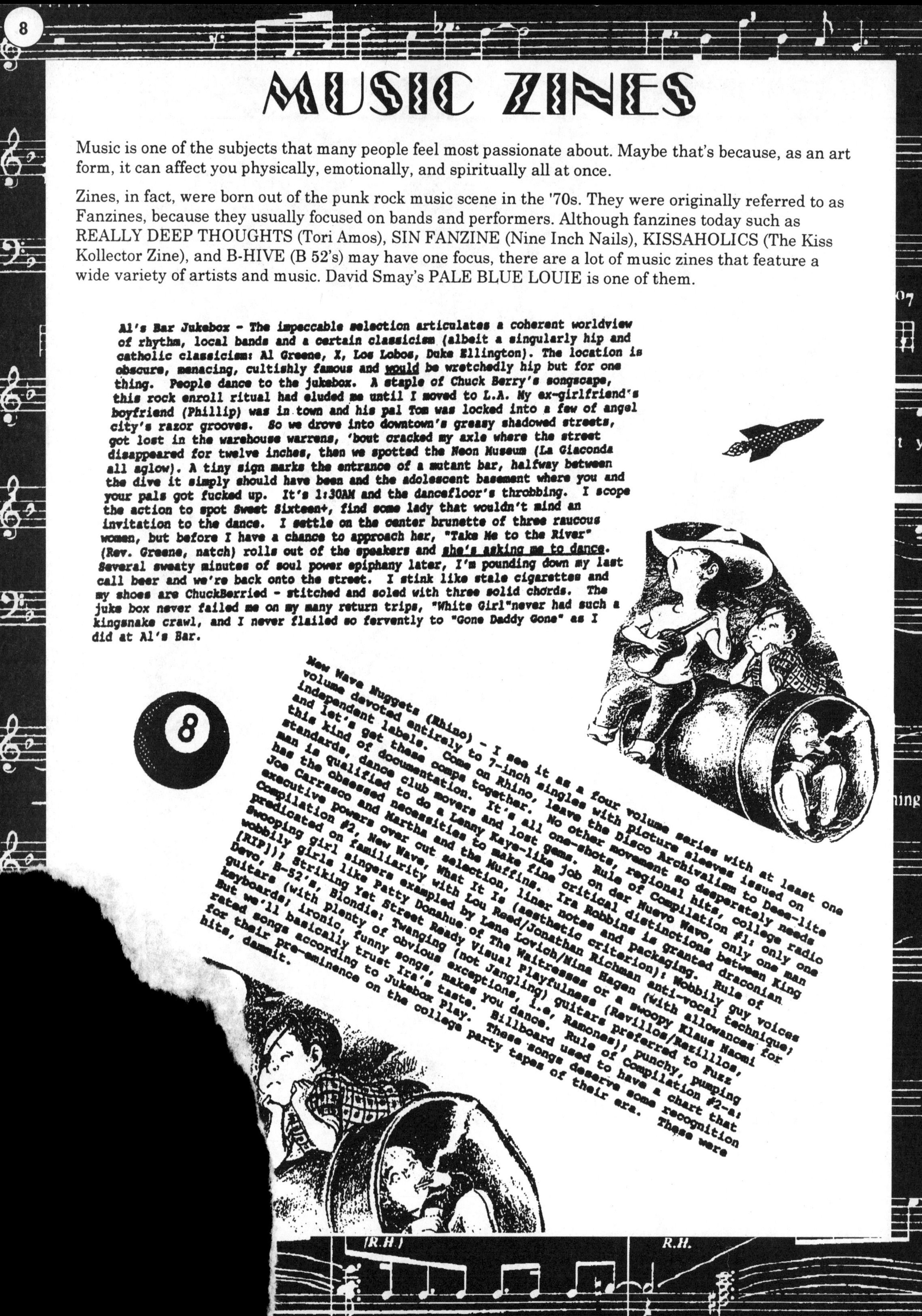

Al's Bar Jukebox - The impeccable selection articulates a coherent worldview of rhythm, local bands and a certain classicism (albeit a singularly hip and catholic classicism: Al Greene, X, Los Lobos, Duke Ellington). The location is obscure, menacing, cultishly famous and would be wretchedly hip but for one thing. People dance to the jukebox. A staple of Chuck Berry's songscape, this rock enroll ritual had eluded me until I moved to L.A. My ex-girlfriend's boyfriend (Phillip) was in town and his pal Tom was locked into a few of angel city's razor grooves. So we drove into downtown's greasy shadowed streets, got lost in the warehouse warrens, 'bout cracked my axle where the street disappeared for twelve inches, then we spotted the Neon Museum (La Giaconda all aglow). A tiny sign marks the entrance of a mutant bar, halfway between the dive it simply should have been and the adolescent basement where you and your pals got fucked up. It's 1:30AM and the dancefloor's throbbing. I scope the action to spot Sweet Sixteen+, find some lady that wouldn't mind an invitation to the dance. I settle on the center brunette of three raucous women, but before I have a chance to approach her, "Take Me to the River" (Rev. Greene, natch) rolls out of the speakers and she's asking me to dance. Several sweaty minutes of soul power epiphany later, I'm pounding down my last call beer and we're back onto the street. I stink like stale cigarettes and my shoes are ChuckBerried - stitched and soled with three solid chords. The juke box never failed me on my many return trips, "White Girl"never had such a kingsnake crawl, and I never flailed so fervently to "Gone Daddy Gone" as I did at Al's Bar.

New Wave Nuggets (Rhino) - I see it as a four volume series with at least one volume devoted entirely to 7-inch singles with picture sleeves issued on independent labels. Come on Rhino, leave the Disco Archivalism to Deee-lite and let's get these comps together. No other movement so desperately needs this kind of documentation. It's all one-shots, regional hits, college radio standards, dance club movers and lost gems. Rule of Compilation #1: only one man is qualified to do a Lenny Kaye-like job on der Nuevo Wavo, only one man has the obsessed necessities to make fine critical distinctions between King Joe Carrasco and Martha and the Muffins. Ira Robbins is granted draconian executive powers over cut selection, liner notes and packaging. Rule of Compilation #2, New Wave, What It Is (aesthetic criterion): Wobbily guy voices predicated on familiarity with Lou Reed/Jonathan Richman anti-vocal technique; Swooping girl singers exampled by Lene Lovich/Nina Hagen (with allowances for wobbily girls like Patty Donahue of The Waitresses or a swoopy Klaus Naomi [RIP]); Striking Yet Street Ready Visual Playfulness (Revillos/Rezilllos, Devo, B-52's, Blondie: Twanging (not Jangling) guitars preferred to Fuzz guitars (with plenty of obvious exceptions, i.e, Ramones); punchy, pumping keyboards; ironic, funny songs, makes you dance. Rule of Compilation #2-a: But we'll basically trust Ira's taste. Billboard used to have a chart that rated songs according to Jukebox Play. These songs deserve some recognition for their pre-eminence on the college party tapes of their era. These were hits, dammit.

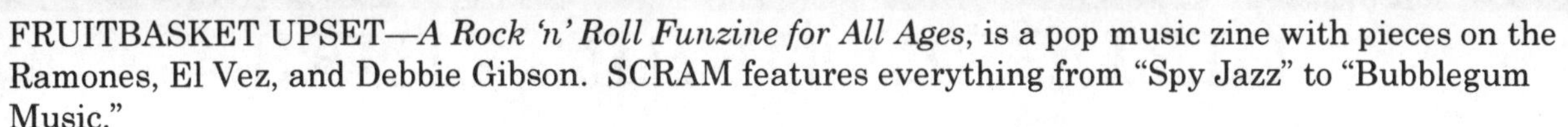

FRUITBASKET UPSET—*A Rock 'n' Roll Funzine for All Ages*, is a pop music zine with pieces on the Ramones, El Vez, and Debbie Gibson. SCRAM features everything from "Spy Jazz" to "Bubblegum Music."

over by a benign Hefneresque figure is raised in this lyric from "1910 Cotton Candy Castle": "Here comes the Lollipop Man in his goody ship Lollipop/ All aboard for lollipop land where the lovin' never stops." *Mm-hmmm, mister, this thing tastes good!*

The Archies' "Sugar Sugar" (#1, Billboard, September 1969), pretty much the only bubblegum hit that still turns up regularly on oldies radio, has one of the sexiest moments this side of Tim Buckley when the anonymous vocalist (Archie? Reggie? Ron Dante?) explodes, "Like the summer sunshine, pour your sweetness over me." These are the same Archies who celebrated bestiality in their non-hit "Hot Dog." It's always seemed suspicious that a gang of kids would name their canine mascot Hot Dog, but this is worse than anyone could have imagined.

Hot Dog, life is tastin' pretty good, oh yeah
Hot Dog, 'cause you love me like you should, oh yeah
So put some mustard on my roll
'Cause you're barking up my soul, Hot Dog
Hot Dog, feel like kickin' up my heels
Hot Dog, oh how good your kissing feels, oh yeah
So wag your tail and let me know
Just how much you love me so, Hot Dog...
I really relish you
Who could embellish you?

The Archies were masters at evoking the nervous excitement of adolescent sexuality. Reggie's menacing "Don't Touch My Guitar" is directed at his room-cleaning mother, and the titular "guitar" is clearly a symbolic stand-in for less savory items hidden in his bedroom. "Kissin'," with its Who-inspired stutter, sums up everything you need to know about what really went on at Riverdale High: "When you're feeling sad and blue, kissin' is the thing to do." There was a dark side to all this experimentation, however: on "Hide and Seek," the traditional children's game is played out as sheer sexual predation, and that old date-raper Reggie sneers, "It's an old game with a brand new twist/ Whoever gets caught is gonna get kissed" — at least!

HOT DOG

THE Archies
FULL FIDELITY 33⅓ RPM
KIRSHNER RECORD

And so things might have continued indefinitely, with new and goofier bands spring up to service each fresh generation of tykes, had not the creative team of Hanna-Barbera and Sid and Marty Krofft conspired to take things entirely too far. They shamelessly developed and

Ignite only under strict parental supervision.

page 69

Excerpt from piece by Kim Cooper. SCRAM #5

If you write about music, try to make your reader sweat, shake, and cry—the way you do when you hear your favorite song!

GIRL/GERL/GRRRL ZINES

Riot Grrrls are empowering themselves, and each other, by speaking out and fighting back against a society that often disrespects and dismisses women. This powerful support network of angry ("grrr") grrrls is committed to a "REVOLUTION GIRL-STYLE NOW."

GIRLS • GIRLS • GIRLS • GIRLS • GIRLS • GIRLS
FIGHT SIZEISM
You know why? Cuz I rOck!
THEY WANT ME TO BE AN ANGRY GIRL
THEY LIKE ME MUCH BETTER THAT WAY
BUT I DON'T FEEL THEIR RAGE
I DO NOT CARRY THEIR BURDEN
I'LL NEVER BE THE SAME
They want me to be a beautiful girl
They like me much better that way
It's easier to look at a doll than at flesh
I'll never be the same.
They want me to be a perfect girl
They like me much better that way
With no faults or flaws, their fantasy come alive
But I'll never be the same
they want no voice
they want no perception
they want no heart
they do not want me

Zines are an integral part of the girl movement. They can provide a lifeline for their creators that readers can plug into as well.

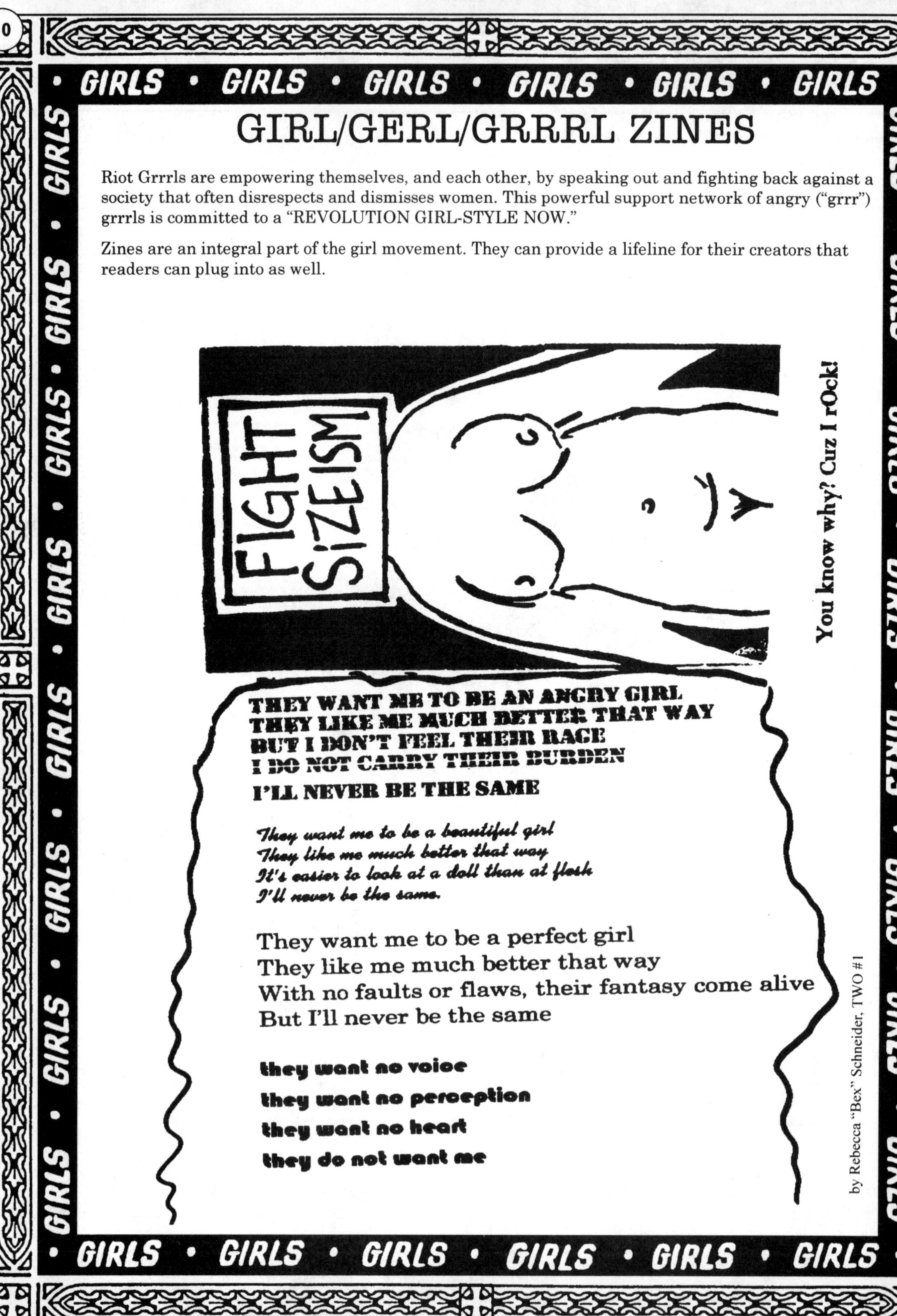

by Rebecca "Bex" Schneider, TWO #1

GIRLS • GIRLS • GIRLS • GIRLS • GIRLS • GIRLS

little girl-child

there is a little girl in this picture who can't possibly be me but she is. she has the same skin with a small mark near her eye. she has shiny brown hair with gold in it and long eyelashes. this little girl loves barbie. she's made her litebrite into a picture of a boy holding his heart out and a girl running for it. her favorite one. if i could make this little girl understand, i'd tell her that's not how it is. i'd tell her not every girl should look like barbie, not every girl gets a boy's heart at seventeen. i'd take away her favorite toys so she wouldn't have these misconceptions. her favorite things would make her strong, make her proud to be a girl, they'd let her draw her own picture instead of following a stupid pattern like litebrite. i'd tell her, if she could understand, that she'll never be this beautiful again and to be happy and never pout. she hates the darkness. she loves annie. she wants another ken doll. she wants to show her mom what she's made and instead she snaps a photo of the little girl. the moment so precise, so rich of her childhood, what makes her up inside. i'd tell her if she could understand to always be proud, get excited, keep a little belly, fall in love constantly but never with boys and stay beautiful, if at all possible.

Tania Rudy, STOOL PIGEON #3

Behind Every Beautiful Woman...

Women seek Cosmetic Surgery to improve and beautify their appearance. Motivated by the inspiration of bringing "inner beauty" to the surface, Dr. Michael Kamper and Dr. Thomas Toohey are creative, artistic surgeons who often work as a team to produce attractive results, which not only endure, but enable a patient's beauty to blossom!

You will often find a team of skilled, artistic plastic surgeons.

Excuse me, sirs, but do not even try to pass off yer little cultural/societal dictations as suggestions, to make yer insinuations look like truth. Because only womyn who are deluded by yer brand of popular bullshit undergo th sik kind of body manipulation so obtusedly and harmlessly referred to as "cosmetic surgery". Real womyn- who must avoid newspapers & magazines if they don't want to be subjected 2 yer attempts @ making us denigrate ourselves- do not buy into this sort of crap. So grrls, becos today is thursday- or tuesday- or sunday... remind yerself how perfekt u r & how u build all yer mannequins based on yer waist & how all th grrls in yer ads look just like u. Throw away all yer magazines, write a pissy expletive-filled letter to guys like this, eat sumthing fattening, & don't ferget 2 tell yer sister how pretty she looks today on yer way out th door.

Nicole Seymour, ODD GRRL OUT #2

GIRLS • GIRLS • GIRLS • GIRLS • GIRLS • GIRLS

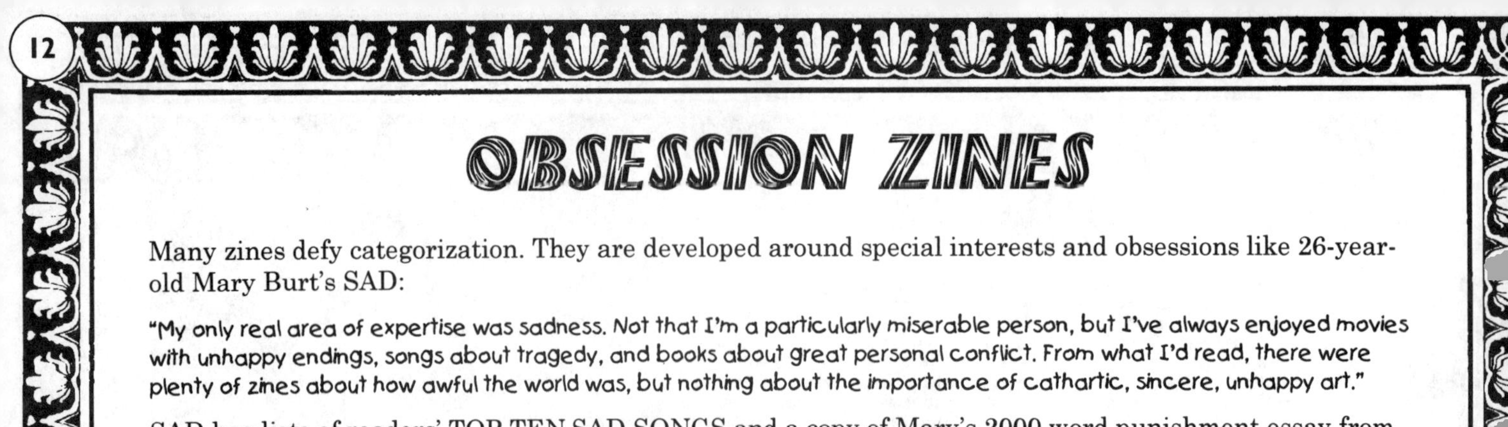

OBSESSION ZINES

Many zines defy categorization. They are developed around special interests and obsessions like 26-year-old Mary Burt's SAD:

"My only real area of expertise was sadness. Not that I'm a particularly miserable person, but I've always enjoyed movies with unhappy endings, songs about tragedy, and books about great personal conflict. From what I'd read, there were plenty of zines about how awful the world was, but nothing about the importance of cathartic, sincere, unhappy art."

SAD has lists of readers' TOP TEN SAD SONGS and a copy of Mary's 2000 word punishment essay from grade school.

NATHANIEL HAWTHORNE.
I first fell in love in the 5th grade. He was a writer, and though he lived far away, I'd seen his photo on the back of one of his books. His high forehead and thick eyebrows emphasized his deep-set, bright eyes. His long, narrow nose and full lips made him seem on the verge of speech. I forced my parents to drive me to his home in Salem, where I learned to my great dismay that my true love was dead.
Sonia, his wife

Also included are SAD games—great mind-benders which have been altered just slightly from their original happy state. . . .

LOGIC PROBLEM CLUES

1. The person who says he's overwhelmed isn't the female who says that she feels isolated and didn't purchase the Metallica album.
2. Though Sylvia feels that high school's a drag, she didn't agree with the person who recently broke up and listens solely to Sebadoh that she's devastated about it.
3. Herve, who doesn't claim to feel unloved, bought a copy of Alannis Morissette's album at the same store where Vincent told the female clerk that he feels paralyzed. He bought the new Offspring record at her recommendation.
4. Kurt feels nagged, but he refuses to say, "Someday, I'll show them."
5. The person who gets no respect is not a female.

* * * * * * * *

	Broke up	No Respect	Unloved	Nagged	High School	Alannis Morrissette	Metallica	Nine Inch Nails	Offspring	Sebadoh	Devastated	Isolated	Overwhelmed	Paralyzed	Vengeful
Kurt															
Vincent															
Savannah															
Sylvia															
Herve															
Devastated															
Isolated															
Overwhelmed															
Paralyzed															
Vengeful															
Alannis Morissette															
Metallica															
Nine Inch Nails															
Offspring															
Sebadoh															

An A to Z of SAD Musical Experiences

A "As Tears Go By" by Marianne Faithfull – I first heard this song when I was about 7. I already felt enough like an old bag lady watching the happy children play. I didn't need this song to tell me that it only gets worse.

B "Baggage Coach Ahead" My dad used to sing this song to me about a father on a train who can't stop his baby from crying. In the song, the other passengers suggest that he take the child to its mother, but, "'If only I could,' the young man replied, 'but she's dead in the coach ahead.'"

C "Chim Chim Chree" by Ray Walston – This was the first sad single I ever owned. For some reason, this part of Mary Poppins made me think that Dick Van Dyke was one of the Beatles.

D Devo "It's a Beautiful World" video – I felt pretty clever for understanding the mock-patriotism of this video, but then I felt so hollow and disturbed that I resented Devo for years for pretending to be a stupid novelty band when actually they were brilliant social critics.

E "Everybody Has Been Burned Before" by the Byrds – An ex-roommate and I made a tape of songs to listen to when depressed about relationships. This was the first song on that tape.

F Fifth Dimension "One Less Bell to Answer" – "I end each day the way I start out, crying my heart out." You don't even need to pine for a lost love to relate to these lines. At least I don't.

G Gloria Gaynor "I Will Survive" – The lyrics to this song were so inspirational to this friendless 8 year old. "As long as I know how to love, I know I'll stay alive."

H "Hanged Man's Dance" by The Singing Loins – The opening verse of this song describes a late night scene with two lovers snuggling together in a park while a dead man hangs from a tree above them. The desolation of the scene reminded me of the time a police officer came to my high school Sociology class to show us slides of teenage boys who had killed themselves by autoerotic asphyxiation. It was part of a series of talks about how immorality and low self-esteem lead to death in teenagers. Other topics included drunk driving and drug addiction.

I "If We're Not Back In Love By Monday" by Merle Haggard – My brother and I got one choice each on the jukebox at Guy's Pizzeria in Louisville. I always picked this song about a guy trying to force his wife to fall in love with him again. My brother always picked the "William Tell Overture."

J Joy Division Closer lp – My favorite cashier at my favorite record store in Louisville used to wear this long-sleeved t-shirt with the Closer album design on the front. I came in one day when he wasn't wearing the shirt and bought the album. He muttered, "Excellent choice," as he rang it up. Imagining him brooding to Ian Curtis's music made me fall in love.

K Karl Hendricks Trio performance, Louisville, Ky – Aaron and I were determined to see Smog perform, so we drove in dangerous weather conditions to a show with only 2 other people in attendance. The band performing when we arrived (Karl Hendricks Trio) sounded perfectly and beautifully miserable. We were moved enough to talk to them afterwards while Smog performed.

L "Lonely In Your Nightmare" by Duran Duran – This is one of those embarrassing songs that you imagine they're singing just to you. Protective songs like this give me hope and make me feel like a disappointment at the same time.

M Martin Denny "Enchanted Sea" – For some reason, this song always gives me the image of my poor cat struggling on a chain gang with a bunch of other delinquent cats.

N Nick Drake St. Nick's Day has special meaning here at Sad headquarters, for it is the day when we honor our patron saint, Nick Drake, who died by overdosing on anti-depressants.

O Olyvia Newton-John "Hopelessly Devoted to You" – I got in trouble once for singing this song at the top of my lungs in my parents' basement. I don't remember who my devotion went to, but I was sincerely upset that it wasn't returned.

P Police "Can't Stand Losing You" – I got this rare single with a cover photo of Sting hanging himself for my 13th birthday. While I was listening to it, my mother received a phone call to tell her that a kid in my class had hung himself.

Q Queen "Bohemian Rhapsody" "Mama, I don't want to die, but sometimes wish I'd never been born at all." Maybe these lines aren't the most brilliant, but they made an impact when I was a kid and heard them for the first time.

R Richman, Jonathan performance, Los Angeles, CA,1995 – Some of the best times in my life, I have to keep completely secret. So, I went to this concert with Aaron and I couldn't tell anyone, because he was too embarrassed to tell his friends that he actually likes Jonathan Richman and that he paid to see him perform live. Fortunately, none of his friends read Sad, so his secret's safe.

S "Spoiled" by Sebadoh – I sat through the entirety of Kids and wasn't struck by any of it as "real" or "moving" until the closing credits rolled and this song came on.

T "Time In A Bottle" performed by Dr. Bensen Honeydew – In this Muppet sketch, Dr. Honeydew drinks different potions as he sings, which make him younger and younger. At the end of the song, he drinks a potion that returns him to his real old age. As the music fades out, we watch him putter around hopelessly.

U Unplugged in New York cd by Nirvana – I admit it. I've listened to this album every day since I've moved to Los Angeles. Each week, I have a new question about song selection or lyrical meaning.

V Victorialand lp by Cocteau Twins – Thinking about this album still reminds me of the first time I heard it. I was alone with this guy who I constantly argued with and who constantly annoyed me. I mistook my aggravation for attraction and spent a miserable month in pursuit of him. I feel gross just talking about it. Needless to say, I never listen to this album any more.

W The Wedding Present – Every painful lyric of jealousy or resentment written by David Gedge has rung so achingly true to my own experience that maybe I'll quit having relationships altogether and just listen to Wedding Present albums to suffer vicariously without having to involve other humans.

X X-mas performance, Skullhead I went to see this local band perform a free all-ages show to celebrate X-Mas, because I knew that this guy that I was in love with would be there. He was, but so was his ex-girlfriend. They got back together that very night.

Y "You Forget to Answer" Nico – I used to bring my Nico tapes on any long journey that Aaron and I would take together in a car. Nico gave him the creeps, so I'd listen to it after he fell asleep. Somehow, this song always struck me as particularly appropriate to that situation, kind of like in that Roger Waters song where he asks, "Are you fast asleep? Good, coz that's the only time when I can really speak to you."

Z Zombies Single As and Bs – This album has a surplus of sad tunes, like "Just Out of Reach," "What More Can I Do," and, "Leave Me Be." Just the titles are enough to break my heart.

THE FREAKIE MAGNET: *A Cereal Funzine*, edited by Kevin Meisner, age 31, explores all aspects of killer cereal culture (not to be confused with serial killer culture).

Why Cereal Boxes?

by Kevin Meisner

OK so it's been two years since I published the first issue of Freakie Magnet. You may recall, in Issue #1, an article by Rocky Flynn entitled "Why Cereal Boxes." In that article, Rocky, a long-time cereal box collector, made very good arguments supporting our hobby. I found the article to be interesting, but at the time I was not interested in cereal boxes at all. I wanted Freakies prizes and that was it. That's what I collected when I was a kid, that's what I had been wanting for all those twenty years, and that's what I got. Literally hundreds of Freakies prizes.

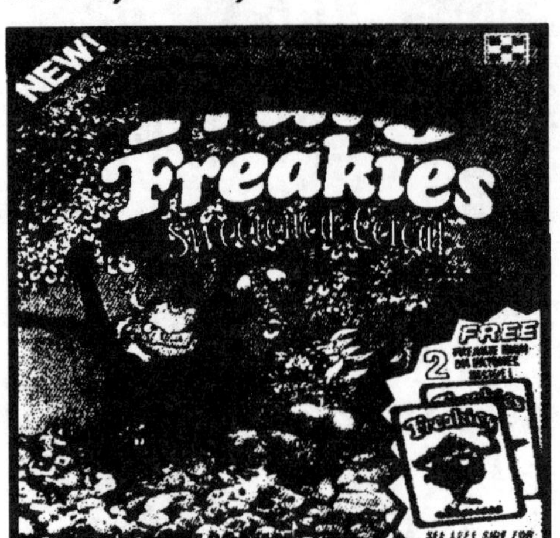

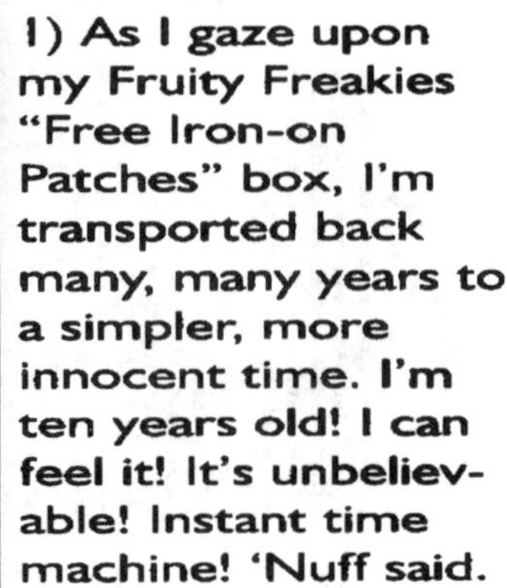

Two years is a long time. I have been exposed (some might say over-exposed) to the most enthusiastic cereal box collectors in the country. I have published EIGHT issues of Freakie Magnet. I have changed.

While I will always cherish my five sets of Freakies plastic figures, my set of Freakies magnets and my set of Freakmobiles, I now conclude that cereal boxes are the ultimate collectible within the realm of cereal collecting. Here's why:

1) CEREAL BOXES ARE NOSTALGIC;
2) CEREAL BOXES ARE RARE;
3) CEREAL BOXES EXIST (AND THAT'S ASTONISHING)!

1) As I gaze upon my Fruity Freakies "Free Iron-on Patches" box, I'm transported back many, many years to a simpler, more innocent time. I'm ten years old! I can feel it! It's unbelievable! Instant time machine! 'Nuff said.

2) Boy am I lucky to have this box! There aren't many of them, certainly not enough to go around. This box was hard to find and the reward is sweet. The search was great fun, and I'm psyched that my enthusiasm, time and effort put this box back into my hands. I'm actually overjoyed! How many are there, five, ten? And I'm one of the only ones who's got one...

3) What the hell is this box doing here? Didn't I cut it, shred it, rip it up into a million tiny pieces and bury it deep within some long-forgotten land fill? Hasn't it deteriorated, disintegrated and evaporated by now? Why is this box here? I just can't believe it!

Get it? Old cereal boxes are nostalgic, rare and shouldn't even exist! It's simple. Cereal boxes are the coolest. Any questions?

With its pale pink cover and kitschy cool artwork, Robyn E. Lee's GIRL DETECTIVE explores the private-eye theme . . . .

EDITORIAL

Hey! All you hot young teens!

So, are you ready to be a Girl Detective? Are you ready to devote your life to sleuthing, ridding the world of even the most difficult mysteries? Are you kids ready to have some fun!?!?!?

I have decided to help out Girl Detectives all over the world with this publication. I will bring to you the latest detective products, true mysteries, and tips from professional spies and detectives . All these things combined will help your sleuthing abilities, and hopefully inspire more teens to try their skills at this exciting lifestyle. So read Girl Detective faithfully, and recommend it to all your friends. And, if you have any great mysteries you would like to share, or any comments on this issue, write to me and tell me all about it! I'll print it in my next issue!

Sincerely,
Robyn E. Lee
Girl Detective Extrordinaire

sleuthing tips for HOT YOUNG TEENS!

When sleuthing in dangerous areas, always try and bring friends along. You never know when you'll need a helping fist. And make sure to bring your flash-light!

Always try to work on friendly terms with your local law enforcement. They may decide to share information with you, and your clues may lead them to their criminals. Once you have established yourself as a top-notch sleuth, they may even offer cases to you when they are stumped. Just like me & Nancy Drew!

Never stop looking for **clues!!!** They are the keys to all mysteries. Don't leave an inch unsearched around the area of your mystery. Even the smallest button may prove to be an important clue!

So if you're a sad, cereal eating sleuth, you can always find a zine to suit you.

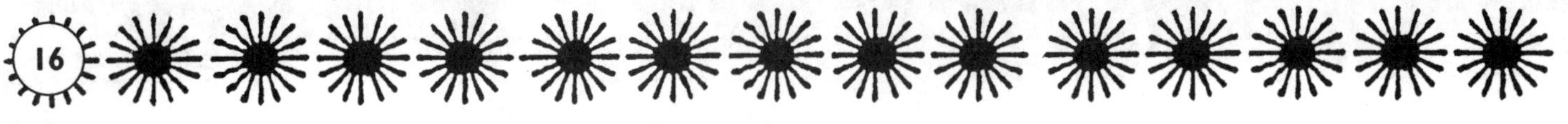

PER-ZINES

Many people write zines featuring journal entries, poems, essays, and letters on abuse, rape, eating disorders, racism, sexism, misogyny, and suicide. What makes these so powerful is that they're the real thing, not like magazines where you flip the page to a glossy image of a skinny model after reading about the rise in cases of anorexia.

Per-zines are devoted to the innermost thoughts and feelings of the zinester. They are often heavy with pain, but the energy of self-expression makes them dance.

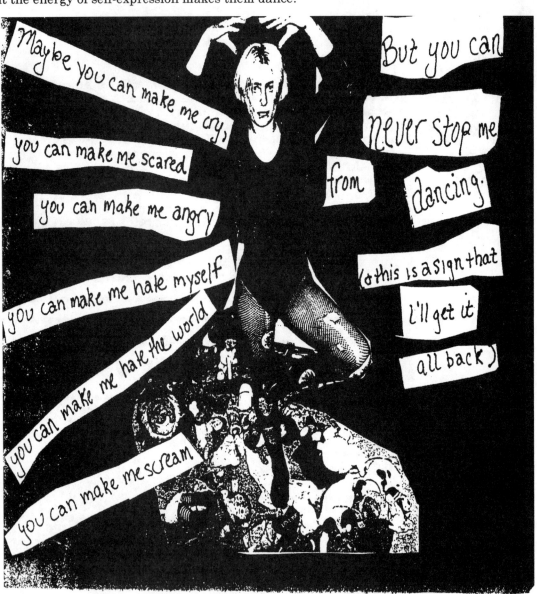

Stephanie Kuhnert, HOSPITAL GOWN

In HOSPITAL GOWN, Stephanie Kuhnert, age 17, works through her suffering from the mental abuse inflicted by a former boyfriend; Tai, age 18, uses her zine CICADA to write about her experience with self-mutilation and how it relates to early incidents of sexual abuse. Other young women, like Jamie Rubin, age 16, of BEAUTIFUL RED LINES and Andrea H., age 15, of SCREAMING MIMI also write about cutting themselves. They speak of their ongoing battles with depression with a lyricism and pain even deeper than the marks they compulsively carve into their skin.

In her zine, LOOKING GLASS GIRL, 18-year-old Melissa Albach confronts her near-death experience after a serious illness—as well as daily internal deaths caused by prejudice—with words that simultaneously slice and soothe.

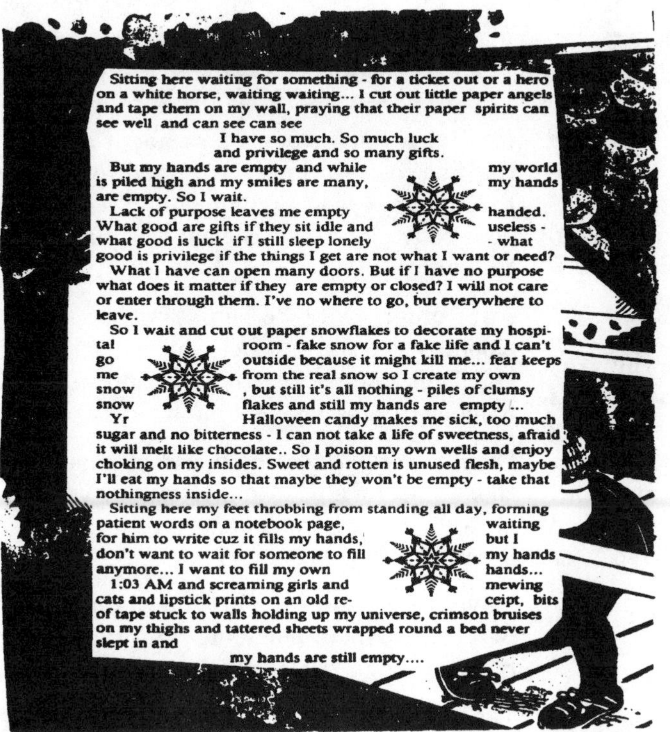

Sitting here waiting for something - for a ticket out or a hero on a white horse, waiting waiting... I cut out little paper angels and tape them on my wall, praying that their paper spirits can see well and can see can see

I have so much. So much luck
and privilege and so many gifts.

But my hands are empty and while my world is piled high and my smiles are many, my hands are empty. So I wait.

Lack of purpose leaves me empty handed. What good are gifts if they sit idle and useless - what good is luck if I still sleep lonely - what good is privilege if the things I get are not what I want or need?

What I have can open many doors. But if I have no purpose what does it matter if they are empty or closed? I will not care or enter through them. I've no where to go, but everywhere to leave.

So I wait and cut out paper snowflakes to decorate my hospital room - fake snow for a fake life and I can't go outside because it might kill me... fear keeps me from the real snow so I create my own snow, but still it's all nothing - piles of clumsy snow flakes and still my hands are empty ...

Yr Halloween candy makes me sick, too much sugar and no bitterness - I can not take a life of sweetness, afraid it will melt like chocolate.. So I poison my own wells and enjoy choking on my insides. Sweet and rotten is unused flesh, maybe I'll eat my hands so that maybe they won't be empty - take that nothingness inside...

Sitting here my feet throbbing from standing all day, forming patient words on a notebook page, waiting for him to write cuz it fills my hands, but I don't want to wait for someone to fill my hands anymore... I want to fill my own hands...

1:03 AM and screaming girls and mewing cats and lipstick prints on an old receipt, bits of tape stuck to walls holding up my universe, crimson bruises on my thighs and tattered sheets wrapped round a bed never slept in and

my hands are still empty....

I WILL TAKE MY SCARS AND WEAR THEM WITH PRIDE - THEY ARE SIGNS OF LIFE AND OF THE BATTLES I HAVE FOUGHT... YOU MAY DISLIKE THEIR SHAPE OR SHADE. OR THE PLACEMENT ON THE FLESH - BUT TO ME THEY ARE THINGS I WORKED HARD FOR. AND THEY ARE MY REMINDER THAT I CAN NOT FORGET WHAT IT TOOK TO GET ME HERE.. AND THEY MAY BE UNSIGHTLY AND MAKE YOU UNCOMFORTABLE. BUT THIS IS MY LIFE AND THESE ARE MY SCARS... AND I WILL WEAR THEM WITH PRIDE & NOT IN SHAME...

When some zinesters feel the need to stray from their basic focus, they make . . .

ONE-SHOT MINIS

Usually quarter size (4 1/4" x 5 1/2") or smaller, these are either distributed separately from the original zine or included as an insert.

Michelle Morgan Cross, (ADVERSARIA and SMUDGE), created WE WERE WEDNESDAY MUSICIANS as an homage to a boy she had a crush on for years, who died suddenly at the age of fifteen. Interspersing diary entries detailing her growing attachment, with newspaper clippings ("Hear Defect Kills Youth"), Michelle's tribute is chilling and haunting.

* * *

Tiny, eerie line drawings tell the story of a family hunting trip, complete with dead deer, flaming houses, and coffee creamers in SPOOKY'S CHILD by Gary W. Peterson. Gary even takes the one-shot idea a step further by including a mini within his mini. Fastened on the inside cover by a tiny piece of velcro, BLOWED UP CLOWN is just 1" x 2"!

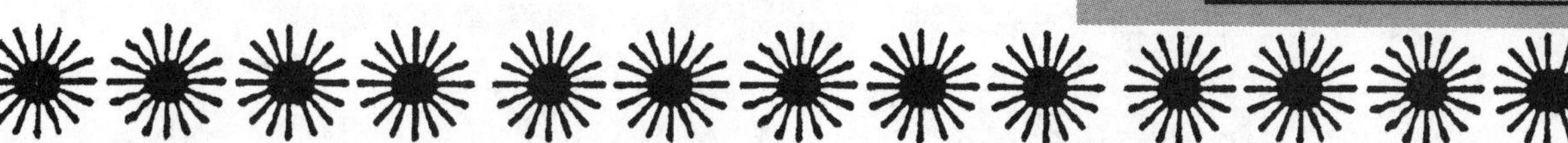

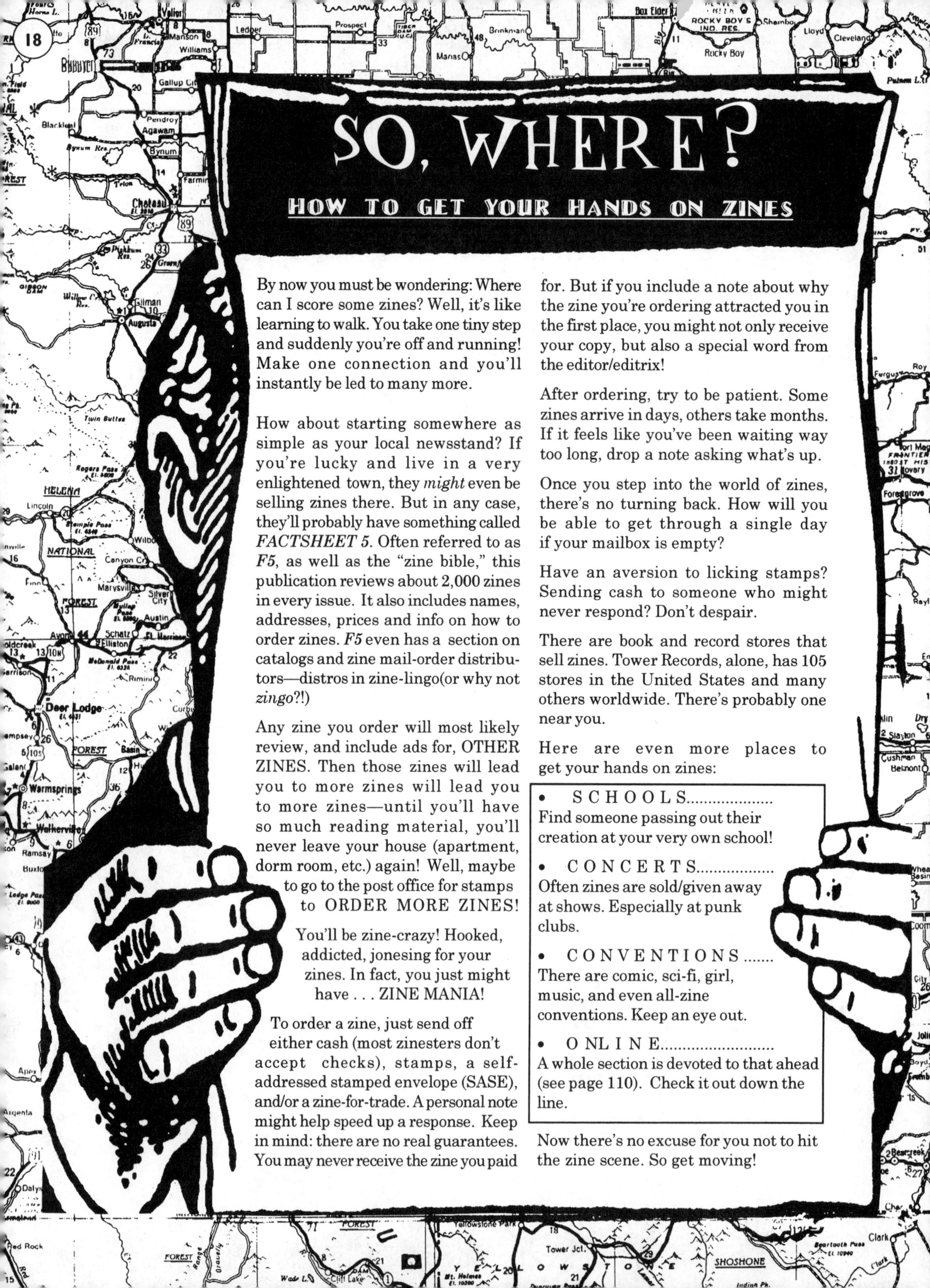

SO, WHERE?

HOW TO GET YOUR HANDS ON ZINES

By now you must be wondering: Where can I score some zines? Well, it's like learning to walk. You take one tiny step and suddenly you're off and running! Make one connection and you'll instantly be led to many more.

How about starting somewhere as simple as your local newsstand? If you're lucky and live in a very enlightened town, they *might* even be selling zines there. But in any case, they'll probably have something called *FACTSHEET 5*. Often referred to as *F5*, as well as the "zine bible," this publication reviews about 2,000 zines in every issue. It also includes names, addresses, prices and info on how to order zines. *F5* even has a section on catalogs and zine mail-order distributors—distros in zine-lingo(or why not *zingo*?!)

Any zine you order will most likely review, and include ads for, OTHER ZINES. Then those zines will lead you to more zines will lead you to more zines—until you'll have so much reading material, you'll never leave your house (apartment, dorm room, etc.) again! Well, maybe to go to the post office for stamps to ORDER MORE ZINES!

You'll be zine-crazy! Hooked, addicted, jonesing for your zines. In fact, you just might have . . . ZINE MANIA!

To order a zine, just send off either cash (most zinesters don't accept checks), stamps, a self-addressed stamped envelope (SASE), and/or a zine-for-trade. A personal note might help speed up a response. Keep in mind: there are no real guarantees. You may never receive the zine you paid for. But if you include a note about why the zine you're ordering attracted you in the first place, you might not only receive your copy, but also a special word from the editor/editrix!

After ordering, try to be patient. Some zines arrive in days, others take months. If it feels like you've been waiting way too long, drop a note asking what's up.

Once you step into the world of zines, there's no turning back. How will you be able to get through a single day if your mailbox is empty?

Have an aversion to licking stamps? Sending cash to someone who might never respond? Don't despair.

There are book and record stores that sell zines. Tower Records, alone, has 105 stores in the United States and many others worldwide. There's probably one near you.

Here are even more places to get your hands on zines:

- SCHOOLS..................
Find someone passing out their creation at your very own school!
- CONCERTS.................
Often zines are sold/given away at shows. Especially at punk clubs.
- CONVENTIONS ....
There are comic, sci-fi, girl, music, and even all-zine conventions. Keep an eye out.
- ONLINE........................
A whole section is devoted to that ahead (see page 110). Check it out down the line.

Now there's no excuse for you not to hit the zine scene. So get moving!

WELL, WHO?

There is a zine drawn by a seven-year-old boy (CHARACTER COMICS); one zine includes pieces by three generations of women, the oldest of whom is 85 (RED GERANIUMS AND BANANA PEELS). Casandra Melee Stark does COOCOOLOCO with a group of mentally disabled adults, and DUPLEX PLANET's David Greenburger features writing by Senior Citizens. Fat boys and girls write zines about just that, as do owl collectors, bowling enthusiasts, and heliophobes.

As long as you have a pen and some paper, you're set. It doesn't have to cost much more than that. Of course you can always spend more money on photocopying, mailing, getting a P.O. Box (to avoid giving out your home address), etc. But the point is ANYONE can do a zine. If you are young, old, rich, poor, serious, humorous, pissed off, all a-giggle, sXe—(straight edge), decadent, cute, scary, introverted, extroverted, ambitious, laid back, hetero-homo-omni-ambi-pan-or-undecidedly sexual, *whatever*—you can make a zine as individual as you are and put it out there.

You don't have to be a writer, or an artist, or have something earth-quaking to say.

Let's meet some zinesters who make everything they say resonate.

EmilieFeingold-Tarrant

GIRL INFINITY'S thirteen-year-old 'Electra Karma' says her mother Shira, also known as 'Lady Swan', works on the zine just as much as Emilie does plus, "she does all the driving."

Here's why Emilie zines: "If I have to sit another day being told I can talk, but I have to wait my turn (which is never) and I have to do it quietly, I'm gonna lose it. I'm not gonna wait to be heard."

Maybe zine-ing is in Emilie's genes—not only passed down from her mother: "My great grandfather had a couple of zines, only they were called small presses then."

At the end of the movie, Apramian and Kyle came to the theater for question and answer. I was the lucky one. I approached Apramian and handed her a copy of Girl Infinity, hot off the press. It was power. It was my creation, being respected by another creator. From one creator to another. Equals. No one was better than the other. She directed a movie that I saw. I published a zine that she read. We both created art. We both created information. A release. An outlet. A media. A form of reaching endless numbers of people. Our own way of yelling, screaming, babbling. Our own way to make noise, be heard. Our own way to yell at the top of our lungs, do something, change this shit.

Excerpt from piece in GIRL INFINITY #3; illustration by Andy Warthog

ZINESTER PROFILES

ROBIN CRANE

SWEETHEART, by Robin Crane, is full of pretty grrrly images like dolls, faeries, angels, hearts, flowers, doves, lace, butterflies, bunny rabbits, and movie goddesses. But it's also got hard-edged comix, scary tarot cards, Axl Rose and The Red Hot Chili Peppers raves/rants, Kurt Cobain laments, and original punk song lyrics. In fact, it's sort of a punk Victorian valentine.

What has been fascinating about SWEETHEART is to see its metamorphosis from shimmery cocoon to fearsome flying creature. The first issue was done in 1992 when Robin was 13 years old, and she's still at it. The early SWEETHEARTs had lots of delicate poems, so ethereal they could almost float off the page, as well as neon teacup blackberry lipstick dreams of living in a Hollywood cottage, thrift-shop furnished and a-dazzle with Christmas lights at all seasons. There were fantasies of mohawked boyfriends, glam urban romps in feather boas, and gala slumber parties.

Robin wrote about her mom ("a Rossetti painting tangled in rose water"), her friends ("Adi loves Sid Vicious and Hollywood and doesn't like bread . . . She doesn't know she's wondrous. And everyone should know that they are wondrous"), and the city she lives in: ——————→

This is my token song about L.A.
here is the reason i wish i could pray
so i could ask god to flood it away
wake up children, we're still here today.

This is L.A. where i scream and i spit
and i live among devils
and walk in their shit
and i live among angels
and bite off their wings
and i tear off their halos
and steal all their things.

This is L.A. where my life turned to flowers
and i turned super hero and won super powers
but then i was chained
to the sky scraper towers
and they plowed up my pride
with their new bloody plowers.

This is L.A. with its Chinatown
with its Melrose, Watts Towers,
all faded and brown.
i'll fade here too,
in my grin and my gown
and i'll laugh and i'll dance
as it all crumbles down.

This is L.A., there are no movie stars
no people to save you in shiny white cars
we all just get drunk in world famous bars
we bleed all our wishes
and store them in jars.

51

LA PALMA

FARMERS MARKET

Between issue #1 and issue #3 of SWEETHEART, there were some subtle transformations. For example, check out "JOCELYN'S ROOM":

JOCELYN'S ROOM

ON THE WALL: 83 PICTURES OF GUNS N' ROSES, 3 PICTURES OF L7, 12 PICTURES OF KISS, 4 PICTURES OF NIRVANA, 103 PICTURES OF MÖTLEY CRÜE, 7 PICTURES OF PEARL JAM, 1 OUTSTANDINGLY BEAUTIFUL SEX PISTOLS POSTER.

ON THE FLOOR: 3 BOTTLES OF NAIL POLISH, 38 LETTERS FROM FRIENDS, 13 SODA CANS OR BOTTLES, 4 PLAID SHIRTS, 12 SHOES {including my own}, 15 MAGAZINES, 4 COLORING BOOKS, 1 RED "WHERE'S WALDO" LUNCHBOX.

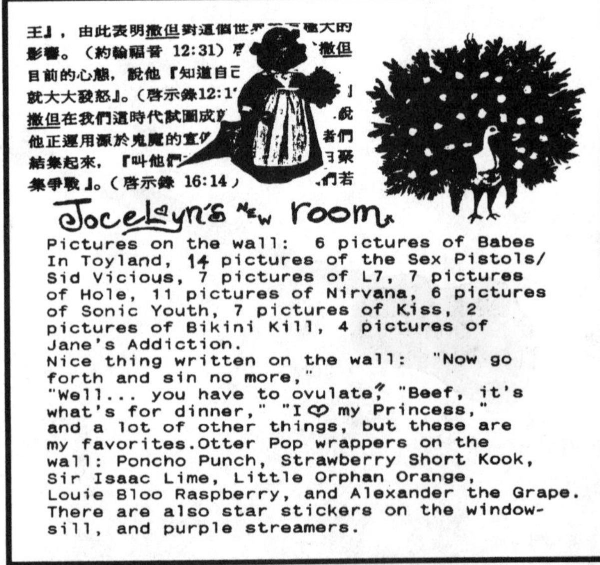

王』，由此表明撒但對這個世
影響。（約翰福音 12:31）
目前的心態，說他『知道自
就大大發怒』。（啓示錄12:1
撒但在我們這時代試圖成
他正運用源於鬼魔的宣
結集起來，『叫他們
集爭戰』。（啓示錄 16:14）

Jocelyn's New room

Pictures on the wall: 6 pictures of Babes In Toyland, 14 pictures of the Sex Pistols/ Sid Vicious, 7 pictures of L7, 7 pictures of Hole, 11 pictures of Nirvana, 6 pictures of Sonic Youth, 7 pictures of Kiss, 2 pictures of Bikini Kill, 4 pictures of Jane's Addiction.
Nice thing written on the wall: "Now go forth and sin no more," "Well... you have to ovulate," "Beef, it's what's for dinner," "I ♡ my Princess," and a lot of other things, but these are my favorites.Otter Pop wrappers on the wall: Poncho Punch, Strawberry Short Kook, Sir Isaac Lime, Little Orphan Orange, Louie Bloo Raspberry, and Alexander the Grape. There are also star stickers on the window-sill, and purple streamers.

A few years later, when Robin was playing with her band, something happened that radically altered her life *and* her work:

This is a true story about punk rock and gang violence and why i'm afraid of noise

hey, it's me. the little bitch. remember? were you too drunk that night to remember my face? well here it is. notice the little red bumps? well that's because i'm only sixteen. notice the space in my eye? well that's where the youthful gleam used to be. do you know what happened to that gleam, motherfucker? it leaked into my bloodstream, and now i'm poisoned, and now i'll only live for seventy years, and that's not nearly enough time to forget the smell of your boot on my face. was it you? was it you? it was you. congratulations to you, on your thorough job on me. now i'm just as stupid and mean and **hateful** as you. now i laugh at every beautiful thing i once created. now i create ugly. i used to be a poet, not a death-threat writer. congratulations, i'm as awful as you now. and if i had the chance i would hurt you as bad as you hurt me, i would skin you and then i would saw off all your muscles and you would just be bones. i would bury you in my back yard. oh fuck, what happened? to me. wait, i forgot- it's no big deal. it's just a game you play with mice. it's not my whole life rotting. it's just a story for newsmen to chuckle at. just talking bout my generation. i forgot that "shit happens." what a joke. do you know what i really dream of every night? i dream that we're all friends and that i'm part of your gang and that you never made me bleed. that's my real secret wish, that i could be a part of the kill-machine. the real-machine. the ruler of my life.

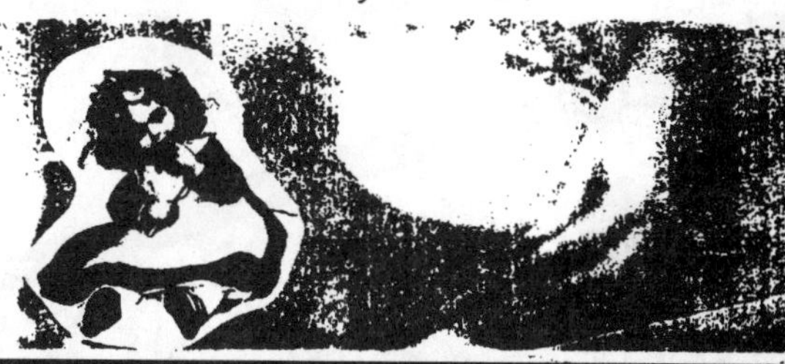

Robin says: "Ever since I got attacked, I find that most of my writing is in some way about that experience. . . usually I get the most real inspiration to write when I've been thinking about the attack."

Now her poetry is sometimes bitter and angry, but stronger than ever, evolving into longer pieces that are almost short stories. "I usually don't put my more whimsical . . . poetry in my zine," Robin says. "With SWEETHEART, I'm mostly interested in releasing a lot of my anger/self-doubt."

Robin's taken her pain and used it fearlessly to help her feel better—while simultaneously giving us something to hold, admire, and mail to our friends. She shows us that you can be furiously pissed off at what sucks, and still be a sweetheart.

GARY W. PETERSON

Thirty-four-year-old Gary W. Peterson, who has a Bachelor of Fine Arts degree from the University of Wisconsin, River Falls, was laid off from his job designing T-shirts. He was then hired at a fast food restaurant as a "Maintenance Supervisor," and has used his five years of experience there to serve as inspiration for his zine, FAST FOOD JANITOR.

Gary draws with an almost manic intensity, filling notebooks and covering yards of used receipt tape with sketches of co-workers, friends, murder weapons throughout history (including lead pipe, processed cheese, and the disco shoe), plus anything else that crosses his path.

All the drawings in this issue I've done on the leftover register tape rolls that would otherwise get thrown away. So the way to "read" the drawings are in 2 columns per page. top to bottom, top to bottom. They range from underwear ads to restaurant supply catalog images to being so bored that I hid out in the dumpster trying reinterpret the circle.

Gummi Babes

MOMENTS IN LIFE: BREEDERS

He also reveals some of the stranger, behind-the-scenes aspects of life as a Fast Food Janitor—such as the types of injuries co-workers have received—and draws their various "ass widths," which unfortunately took up too many pages to include here!

WHAT I HEARD THE CUSTOMER SAY	WHAT THE CUSTOMER ACTUALLY SAID
HI-G	iced tea
I've got the hots	I need a Boss
cinnamon fries	2 number fives
kick it!	chicken
2 big goats	2 big roasts
2 technicals	2 chocolate cones
ketchup toes	texas toast
tender toes	texas toast
2 flexing blacksticks	2 texas breakfasts
bra, socks inside of boxes	a big side of texas sauce
I want to carry the olympic flame	I want a chicken fillet
mega rubber please circle	bacon double cheeseburger
twist cone	frisco
frisco	twist cone
french horn	twist cone or frisco
incest	texas
greasy trombone	cheeseburger combo

The Fast Food Janitor says, "I try to keep this crappy job as small a part of my life as possible. I spend the rest of the day pursuing my passion of being an artist."

His drawings practically slash and burn off the page, demonstrating how even the most frustrating of situations can be used to create heart-powered art for others to trip on.

SETH BOGARD

Seth Bogard, age 16, has so many zines that you might have trouble deciding what to call him. He could be:

- Seth Applebee or Seth Baskets—for A DAY IN THE LIFE OF APPLEBEE'S, also known as THE CHICKEN FINGERS BASKETS zine
- Seth Been—for BEENS FOR TEENS, which he now co-writes with its original creator, Liz. (He calls it "total teen star porno trash . . . . My mom really hates it. It's the raddest to make.")
- Seth Hero—after HEROES FOR TODAY, his zine distro catalog ("Teenagers should be the heroes for today.")
- Seth PUBERTY STRIKE ("I'm sick of puberty and I'm going to do something about it so I can stay 16 for the rest of my life.")
- Seth DIORAMA (a now-defunct zine he did with Layla Rose Cooper)

Seth makes it simple. He says his only zine aliases are Seth Bee or Seth Baskets. Whatever you call Seth, you can be sure of one thing: He's a kooky "teenybopper" (his word) and proud of it.

Whether he and Liz are decorating BEENS FOR TEENS with a glued-on, uncooked "penis-pasta" noodle, or he's listing the things that make him "wanna cry" (The Wizard of Oz and poodle poachers), Seth, who has made about 30 issues of his 5 or 6 different zines in just 3 years, is a self-proclaimed "RETARD ZINE MACHINE."

Here's some stuff Seth has to say about his zine mania:

A DAY IN THE LIFE OF APPLEBEE'S: "In 8th grade I discovered this restaurant called APPLEBEE'S and I was super-obsessed with it. I am an obsessive person. During my freshman year in high school I started my own Applebee's zine. I would write about my experiences there (mostly lies) like Undercover Applebee's, the staff, the food, mainly the CHICKEN FINGERS BASKETS . . . My brother gave my first issue to the Applebee's manager and I got all scared, but he actually liked it and gave me free dessert. He said I had 'too much free time on my hands.' . . . Applebee's also sent me a huge box of presents/money for my Applebee's efforts."

HAIKUS FOR THE APPLEBEE'S YOUNGSTER

To make a good drink,
take a little bit of milk
and mix with Pepsi.

I saw Chevy Chase
Chompin on Chicken Fingers
from the Kid's Menu.

Who ever smelt it
they must have also dealt it
Granny Solitaire.

I'm burning rubber
yeah you just eat my dust, I'll
get you Chevy Chase.

Like his self-portrait, Seth's writing is cheek-tongued and goofily slick.

THE ODDEST ZINE-RELATED THING THAT'S HAPPENED TO HIM: "I almost got beat up like 5 times for my zine by these stupid assholes at my high school. Of course they were all talk."

THE COOLEST ZINE-RELATED THING THAT'S HAPPENED TO HIM: "I almost got beat up like 5 times for my zine."

WHAT'S IMPORTANT FOR HIM TO EXPRESS IN HIS ZINE: "I say what I want to say and what I want to read. I never rant too much about things that have been said a billion times. I get bored with all that crap. Express what you feel and make things honest instead of trying to sound all cool. Nobody thinks I'm cool at all so I don't pretend."

We think you're slinkster cool, Seth.

Seth's teachers, reviewed

1. Mr. [blacked out]: Bilogy, first period. Before I ever saw him I just knew he'd be one of those hard-rockin' Celtic men. Atleast I was hoping so. Turns out he's some kind of sports coach. He's done what no one else has ever done before, he showed me a human brain. It was looking like tuna. I was feeling hot. Mr. G was looking nervous. He wouldn't let me touch it so I give him **Eight stars.**

2. Ms. [blacked out]: English, second period. She claims to be the "meanest teacher in the world." She's really not, but I admire her for trying. She would recieve ten stars but she makes me pay $1 for saying "shut up." **Nine stars.**

3. Mr. [blacked out]: Photo, third period. He makes me laugh when I see the picture of him as a black belt. But he told people I drive him nuts. Maybe it's because I always ask him to play the "Roseanne" theme song on his harmonica. Or maybe because I try to make him look at me wearing Terminator sunglasses. I don't know. **Six stars.**

4. Mr. [blacked out]: Guitar, fourth period. Mr. [blacked out] is a nice man. He is currently cutting a record, or so I've heard through the grapevine. He plays his clarinet along with the kids guitar when they can't play very well. But never for me, maybe that's a compliment. But still, I want to jam with one of my favorite teachers. Just the other day he made us sign a paper saying "students do not sit on the floor." I don't know why. **Nine stars.**

5. Sister [blacked out]: Religion, fifth period. Sad but true, I go to a Catholic school. At home we aren't Jesus followers, but I'm learning to be at school. "Grin and bear it, Seth." (Oh I'm smiling.) Sister [blacked out] truly is the meanest teacher in the world, well besides Ms. [blacked out] who likes to throw desks and staplers. Sister [blacked out] uses a microphone cause she's old and fragile. But she sure doesn't need that microphone when she's yelling her head off. **No Stars.**

6. Mr. [blacked out]: Geometry, sixth period. Besides the fact that Geometry is the worst subject ever invented, Mr. [blacked out] is the only one to get 10 stars. I'll probably be him when I grow up, that's how scary it is. On Halloween he dressed up like Sherlock Holmes. And for fun he lets us try on all his ties and listen to reggae. Plus he's dyslexic, plus he's got a stamp of his own head. **Ten stars.**

(ZINE SCENE felt obliged to black out the names to avoid the wrath of Seth's teachers).

Definitive Guide to (Some of) Seth's Favorite Monsters:

Ro-Man: Starred in the 1953 four star film *Robot Monster*. Ro-man is half man, half monster and is from the moon. His special powers are his extreme strength and deadly calcinator ray. He is sent to kill all earthlings. But like any man would, he has trouble killing a pretty young lady. Only 5 earthlings survive, but it all turns out the whole movie is a young boy's dr^am. Or is it? Rumors of Ro-man sightings after the filming were heard, but no one knows the truth. One of my current favorite films. Add bonus points- it's in 3-D! ←

The Creature from the Black Lagoon: Most of you should know who he is, but if not learn now. Starred originally in 1954's *Creature from the Black Lagoon*. As a smash hit, two sequels followed: *Revenge of the Creature* (in 3-D) and *The Creature Walks Among Us*. His special power is his enormus strength. He is also impervious to spears and bullets. Scientists dig him up and he comes to life. Then dies and comes back to life in the sequels, etc. Then is discovered to be somewhat human. In the end he just escapes without another sequel. Even though I always thought the Creature was a cool monster, the only times he really seemed to scare me was when he would get all horny with the ladies. →

The Alligator Man: Starred in the 1959 film *The Alligator People*. Paul Webster played this six-foot tall mutant with human body and alligator head. His special powers are his extreme strength and powerful alligator jaws. Humans are injected a hormone found in alligators to heal them. But a year later they turn into alligators. It may not seem to brilliant to all you special effects movie genius' out there today, but back then it was something special. ←

The Spider: Starred in the 1958 top-notch film *Earth vs. the Spider*. His special powers are obvious, he's a giant spider. No special tricks like breathing fire or shooting fireballs, nonetheless, he manages to give me a good scare. Sometimes I feel like picking up spiders, other times I feel like running from them. Well, the Spider would definetely make me chose the second if I encountered him. Two square teenagers discover the spider. no one believes them. Until the big bad spider gives them some of their own medicine. He dies in the end after electrocution and dynamite, but gets in a few good kills → beforehand.

She-Monster: Starred in the 1962 film *The Astounding She-Monster*. Her special powers are that she can glow. And when she glows she can kill you with her fingertip. She also walks backwards out of rooms and is bulletproof. I guess you could say "low-budget" special effects, but still definetely one of my favorite movies. Just watching her walk around glowing turns me on. She eventually is killed when a man throws acid at her, but she lives in the hearts of Americans. ←

The Saucer Men: Starred in the 1957 film *Invasion of the Saucer Men* which came out after the book "Amazing Stories." They don't really have any special powers and don't kill too many people either. A teenager kills one and puts it in his freezer and the other saucer men get angry and take revenge. Personally I don't like the Saucer Men. They don't have feet, they only make squeeking noises and their heads are way too big for their bodies. But the movie is worth renting, I guess. →

Note to those who live in Tucson: You can rent these movies at a rental place called "Pink Motel." They have the best monster and science fiction films.

LISA MASLOWE

Lisa Maslowe's THE CAT BOX ROOM comic, is full of her friends (real and imagined), her kitties (or "furchildren") Rufus and Gomez, her job at Psycho records, her dreams, magic secrets of Haight street and Golden Gate Park, and odd tales that make you want to climb right inside the frames and play.

Lisa, age 25, says she was inspired to start CAT BOX ROOM after reading COMETBUS by Aaron Cometbus, a zine that is often praised by other zinesters. Her first issue actually started as a letter to Aaron, describing a weird thing that had happened to her when she was putting up fliers for her band.

"I had to illustrate the story in order to better explain it. Then suddenly I just decided to start over again, do the whole thing as a comic, and then Xerox it off in a book. I didn't know about *Factsheet 5* or the zine culture or anything."

Since then, THE CATBOX ROOM has been reviewed in *F5* and *Maximum Rock 'n' Roll* and lots of people write to Lisa saying how much they love it.

"Zines were really a perfect format for me. I had felt that a lot of crazy things had happened to me in my life and I wanted to write about them. However, whenever I just wrote, it seemed like it sounded stupid. My writing wasn't really literary, nor was the content shocking enough to hold up on its own. But comics in a zine format allowed me to tell my life-stories to people who appreciated slice of life, weird little stories in a way that uppity publishers and literary audiences might not.

"I feel the insatiable need to express myself and my opinions, and I guess I figure I might as well publish the stuff instead of hiding it in my journal. Zines are great when you're shy, but all fired up."

No one but Lisa could have made CAT BOX ROOM. It's a pure expression of her. Reading it is like slipping into a miniature bay-windowed, cat-happy world with a funny, sweet, vegan, yoga-loving drummer artist friend as your guide.

WHAT THE DUCKS KNEW

(A true, yet very condensed story)

The sun had been out every day for weeks.

Everything was beautiful; it was spring.

I was in love, quite suddenly, with a boy I'd known for a day or two.

But our first kiss was doomed to be our last. For, the next time we met, he said:

I can't be involved with you after all. Sorry. I have a long-distance girlfriend. I forgot. Oops.

I said:

No problem, bud. It's spring today. Let's go to Golden Gate Park.

We went to the duck pond.

ABRAHAM KATZMAN

On the cover of FLAMING JEWBOY, Abraham Katzman, age 26, proclaims his manifesto: "THOU SHALT NAME THYSELF * THOU SHALT ACCESSORIZE * THOU SHALT WEAR HEELS * THOU SHALT BASH BACK * THOU SHALT ANOINT THYSELF WITH FRAGRANT OILS * THOU SHALT GROW MIGHTY AS A CEDAR IN LEBANON * THOU SHALT COVET THYSELF * THOU SHALT NEVER FORGET * THOU SHALT SING OUT * THOU SHALT FLAME."

From the smiling young boy-child in a plaid shirt, to the mini-skirted, glam dragstress he has become, Abraham projects strength and determination, WITH STYLE!

"Out of my way! I'm going to be a star!"

-flaming jewboy as a boy

Pepper Spray: Locked Out and Looking Good

"Doing a zine gives you the perfect combination of obscurity and fame. Every zinester is Tiny Tim."

photo by Windy Dungan

"I understand the power of self-publishing, of looking at a blank page and knowing it's me who's going to fill it up. There's nothing so sacred about paper or canvases or dead air. We're all here to write, and draw or speak. Doing my zines meant I was taking my 64 pages worth."

Abraham's pages have been part of exhibitions at museums in New York and Seattle. Combining traditional yiddishisms with heavy homoerotic poetry and shoe wisdom, FLAMING JEWBOY is a celebration of life. The title of Abraham's second zine tells it all: I'M OVER BEING DEAD. In a world of gay-bashing, and other expressions of bigotry that often lead to depression, self-hatred, or even suicide for many young queers, these are words that need to be shouted.

TO DRAG MOMMIES EVERYWHERE

by Abraham Katzman

Teach me how to cut apples with a plastic knife and pour and drink and spell words with wooden blocks. Drag mommies are mommies. I did slide my feet into my mom's navy blue high heels. She was a size 7 and the shoes were too big even with me in tube socks so I must've been twelve or thirteen cause my growth spurt came later. Her shoes held my feet nice and felt good to stand on and walk across the family room in. They made me taller and her lipstick was red on my lips and came off with soap. Drag mommies are different than birth mommies though drag mommies will tell you they can give birth too. You don't worry about being caught in girl clothes by your drag mommy say if she gets home from the store early. Drag mommies will lend you their shoes if the fit is right and your outfit needs it. Not like your real mom if you're a boy child. Full on men can be drag mommies too for boy drag like the I. Goldberg sales clerk in Philly when I bought my first Docs. "Have fun boychik" which is Yiddish for young man and I did for three years in those boots. They were blue and blessed. My mommy had nice sweaters white wool with big brown buttons and was Miss Morningstar and got a not so heavy grey statue for a prize in '54 and was a storefront model like when Chocha Fresca and Babalicious were storefront models on Broadway for an hour. Some guy came in and pulled Babalicious' wig off and he's dead now cause drag mommies protect their young and wigs are young and drag mommies lift one ton cars off their trapped gown trails and boas. Drag mommies are adrenalin full when it counts. My drag mommy is the MAC counter and being in the audience of a good show. My drag mommy is knowing drag is a forever old and sacred transformation. Drag mommies are here cause good drag is hard to do and they show how hard is good. Drag mommies are sexy divorcées who don't know shit about playing bridge or canasta or lawn darts. Drag mommies are their own maids and cooks. Famous drag mommies are Julian Eltinge who taught Mae West how to paint her face so fine folks thought she was a man and Barry is Bette's drag mom and Sonny is Cher's and Joan is Bette's and Bette is Joan's and Edith Head gives good costume and Judy is Liza's and Mizrahi is Sandra's and the Pope is Madonna's and Charo is her own. And when drag mommies die they leave their fake titties and true dresses to the daughters and when drag mommies live which is always they show off their Nerf tits and gender clothes and say I'm a girl who made more of herself than anyone else saw and I believe it. And that's who drag mommies are. Believers in unnatural childbirth and painkillers and bunny slippers and spike-heeled ob/gyns in rubber bondage and in-room movies and lots of recuperation and post-birth aerobicizing and chocolate and Soap Opera Digest from the hospital gift shop. Drag mommies know it hurts when you're so in yourself you can't see your fantasy self. Drag mommies say look at your fresh face self. Erma Bombeck died this April of '96. What would she write in her column about her death. The grass is always greener when the plot's paid for or If life is a bowl of cherries what's death or You all go on without me. See Erma's not a suburban mom anymore. There are no suburbs in the afterlife. Suburban kids gotta move on and be drag mommies for the world of alone kids. So we'll all be that crazy aunt who is full of life and takes kids away from bad places for a magical hour or a magical day. Drag mommies say take yourself out of the bad places in your head and it's all crisp and clean and alive in the spotlight in the back bar in the makeshift dressing room in dance club doorways on top of the piano. Yeah you'll sweat and your toes will go numb from the shoes but drag mommies but drag mommies aren't stage moms. Drag mommies know you'll be good. Drag mommies don't push. They embrace. Drag mommies. Drag mommy day. Drag mommy day. Drag mommy day is ours. Drag mommy day and you and me and every pretty thing about us. Drag mommy day.

Published by flaming jewboy press

HARRELL FLETCHER AND ELIZABETH MEYER

*WHO ARE THE **WHIPPER SNAPPER NERDS** AND WHAT ARE THEY TRYING TO TELL US?*

Beaming in messages from other galaxies, revealing deep emotions, and exploring pop culture icons such as Linda Rondstadt and the Brady Bunch, the Whipper Snapper Nerds are students/artists at Creativity Explored, a non-profit art center for developmentally disabled adults in San Francisco. While working on a video project at Creativity Explored, Harrell Fletcher and Elizabeth Meyer "became great fans of certain artists and decided to start this magazine as a way for their work to reach a larger audience."

So far they've produced about 100 copies of each of five issues, which they distribute by word of mouth, through stores like Comic Relief in San Francisco and Berkeley, and out of *F5*. Even though "it's been a money losing venture," Harrell and Elizabeth keep doing WHIPPER SNAPPER NERD "for our own entertainment and for the fun of sharing what we consider to be amazing artwork done by amazing people."

Each of the issues focuses on the work of one artist and includes an interview, photo, and biography. The title was taken from a piece by John McKenzie, "whose work primarily consists of combinations of words and phrases." In issue #3, in which McKenzie is featured, he wrote "Karen Carpenter Whipper Snapper Nerd."

Star Trek: The Three Stooges

Three Datas. O.K.

Three of Diana Troi, Counselor Troi.

Three of her. They are androids.

Three of Beverly. They are androids.

William Riker. Three of him are androids.

Jean Luc Picard, Starship Captain.

Three of him... ANDROIDS!

THIS IS ABOUT RICK, MYSELF, NELSON.

Ricky Nelson, Jr. -- also known as Elvis, Captain Christopher Pike, and sometimes David Jarvey -- was born to career army parents in Tokyo Japan in 1957. At the age of 12, he moved to the Bay Area and currently lives in a group home in San Francisco. Ricky has been an artist at Creativity Explored since 1984. His art work consists of drawings, paintings, textiles, sculpture and site-specific installations. He has starred in several videos, most notably *Star Trek: The New One* and *The Final Frontier*. Also a dedicated musician, Ricky can often be seen playing guitar on the corner of 16th Street and Mission in San Francisco.

This is the second issue of WHIPPER SNAPPER NERD, a publication of work by student/artists at Creativity Explored, a non-profit art center for developmentally disabled adults. This issue features the work of Jimmy Miles. Jimmy was born in 1957 in San Francisco where he currently lives in a group home. Jimmy has been working at Creativity Explored since 1989.

Harrell Fletcher &
Elizabeth Meyer

This is the third issue of WHIPPER SNAPPER NERD, a publication of work by student/artists at Creativity Explored, a non-profit art center for developmentally disabled adults. This issue features the work of John Mc Kenzie. John was born in the Philippines in 1962 and moved to the U.S. in 1964. He currently lives with his parents in San Francisco's Mission District and has been working at Creativity Explored since 1989.

Harrell Fletcher &
Elizabeth Meyer

John Patrick McKenzie

Linda Ronstadt
is a crybaby
Linda Ronstadt
likes a
ice cream

He came from space.
He Looked at me
Like I was a cAt girL.
I meowed. I am a
cAt girl. Look At
my eyes.

This issue of WHIPPER SNAPPER NERD features the work of Barbara Doehrman. Barbara was born in 1947 and currently lives in a group home in San Francisco. She has been working at Creativity Explored since 1985.

DOGS

Buckeye Dog.

Trick Dog

Pointy Dog

Bull Dog

Fashion Style Dog to Love hats

This issue of WHIPPER SNAPPER NERD features the work of Michael Loggins. Michael was born in 1961 and lives with his parents in San Francisco's Portola district. He has worked at Creativity Explored since 1984.

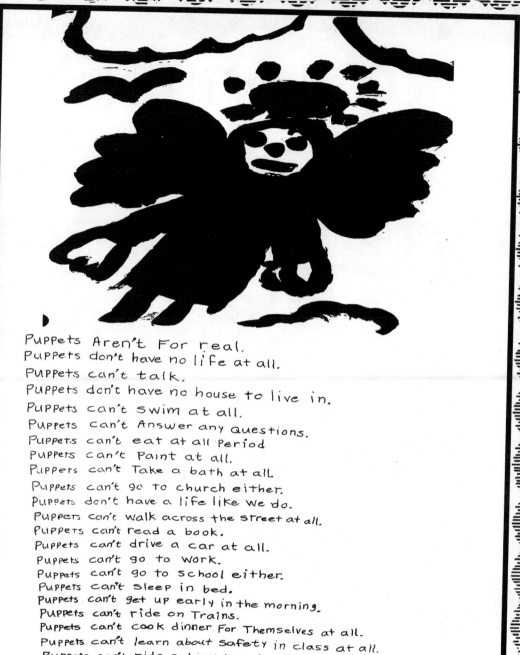

Puppets Aren't For real.
Puppets don't have no life at all.
Puppets can't talk.
Puppets don't have no house to live in.
Puppets can't swim at all.
Puppets can't Answer any questions.
Puppets can't eat at all Period
Puppets can't Paint at all.
Puppets can't Take a bath at all.
Puppets can't go to church either.
Puppets don't have a life like we do.
Puppets can't walk across the street at all.
Puppets can't read a book.
Puppets can't drive a car at all.
Puppets can't go to work.
Puppets can't go to school either.
Puppets can't sleep in bed.
Puppets can't get up early in the morning.
Puppets can't ride on Trains.
Puppets can't cook dinner For Themselves at all.
Puppets can't learn about safety in class at all.
Puppets can't ride a bicycle at all.
Puppets can't Pay to ride on the bus at all.
Puppets can't see where they are going at all Period
Puppets don't know meanings of danger at all.
Puppets don't know the meanings of danger at all.
Puppets don't Take care of Pets.
Puppets can't cross by the light Because can't walk to the light
Puppets can't brush their Teeth at all.
Puppets can't bake a cake at all.
Puppets can't Wash the dishes at all.
Puppets can't change their clothes at all.
Puppets can't sit in the chair by Themselves at all.
Puppets can't Tell The Time at all.
Puppets can't get Theirself in a lots of Trouble at all.

by Micheal Loggins

Of course, what you've seen here is just a teeny sampling of zinesters and their work. There are so many others that deserve in-depth profiles, but we hope you will discover some of your own—and write about them in *your* zine!

FROM WHEN?

A HISTORY OF ZINES

Zines may seem like a relatively new phenomenon, but illustrator David Coulson shows us that there are a few important historical events that prove they've actually been around forever!

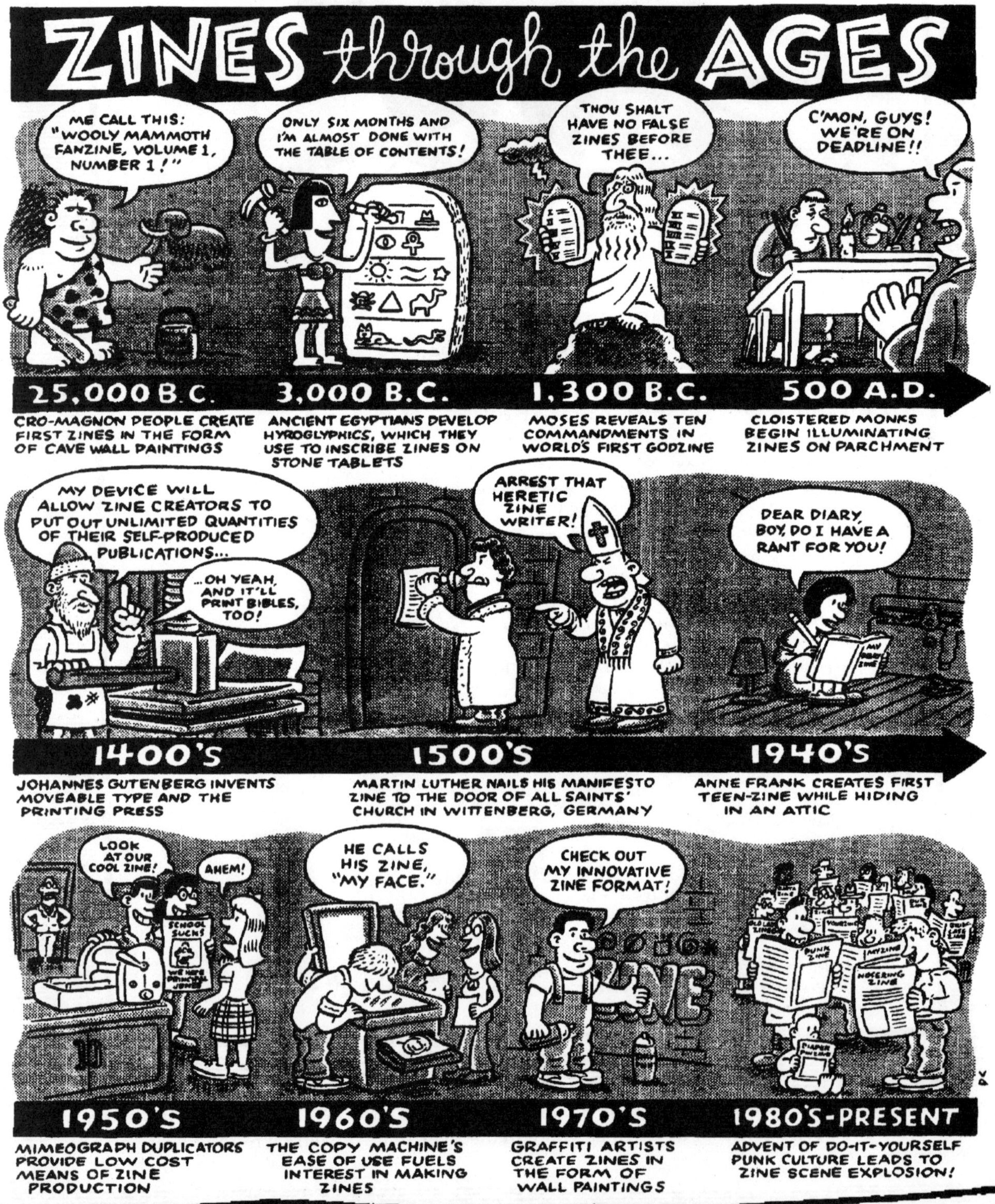

25,000 B.C. CRO-MAGNON PEOPLE CREATE FIRST ZINES IN THE FORM OF CAVE WALL PAINTINGS

3,000 B.C. ANCIENT EGYPTIANS DEVELOP HYROGLYPHICS, WHICH THEY USE TO INSCRIBE ZINES ON STONE TABLETS

1,300 B.C. MOSES REVEALS TEN COMMANDMENTS IN WORLD'S FIRST GODZINE

500 A.D. CLOISTERED MONKS BEGIN ILLUMINATING ZINES ON PARCHMENT

1400'S JOHANNES GUTENBERG INVENTS MOVEABLE TYPE AND THE PRINTING PRESS

1500'S MARTIN LUTHER NAILS HIS MANIFESTO ZINE TO THE DOOR OF ALL SAINTS' CHURCH IN WITTENBERG, GERMANY

1940'S ANNE FRANK CREATES FIRST TEEN-ZINE WHILE HIDING IN AN ATTIC

1950'S MIMEOGRAPH DUPLICATORS PROVIDE LOW COST MEANS OF ZINE PRODUCTION

1960'S THE COPY MACHINE'S EASE OF USE FUELS INTEREST IN MAKING ZINES

1970'S GRAFFITI ARTISTS CREATE ZINES IN THE FORM OF WALL PAINTINGS

1980'S-PRESENT ADVENT OF DO-IT-YOURSELF PUNK CULTURE LEADS TO ZINE SCENE EXPLOSION!

How many people have been involved with zines for almost twenty years? Daniel (Shredder) Weizmann, gives an historical perspective.

THINGS I HAVE ZINE by Shredder

The first zines were probably started by cavemen and cavewomen who carved picture stories about buffalo hunts into rocks and passed them out to their friends. The zine as we know it today hasn't changed all that much—except that they're easier to carry around and pass out to your friends! Zines became popular during the early 1960s, when science fiction fans would send each other short, photocopied, stapled newsletters called **fanzines**.

One sci-fi fan,San Francisco's Greg Shaw, also happened to be a big music fan. He started *The Mojo-Navigator Rock and Roll News*, writing about local groups like the Grateful Dead and the Jefferson Airplane.

Several years later, in the mid-1970s, a new kind of music was brewing and with it, a new exciting fanzine: *Punk*, put out by Legs McNeil and John Holmstrom in New York City. *Punk* covered all the new groups like Blondie, the Ramones, and the Sex Pistols and featured cool photos, collages, gags, and comic strips.

In those days, punk rock music was mostly "underground"—no major record labels would release records by the groups-and no major magazines would write about punk music. People were forced to record and distribute their own music and write about it in "magazines" that they made themselves. These mags were the first punk zines!

The early punk zines had wild, eye-catching names that you couldn't forget: *Search and Destroy, Slash, Lobotomy, Flipside*, and *Damage*. In those days, there were no computer graphics or even word processors! Most of the zines were handwritten or typed, featuring wild, sloppy, glued down collage layouts of ripped out photos and drawings. There were only three rules in those days:

1. Do it YOURSELF!
2. GRAB the reader's attention!
3. ANYTHING goes!

At first, the zines were strictly about the punk music scene: bands, concerts, records, and fashion. But after awhile, some very creative souls—like the people at *Contagion* and *Lowest Common Denominator*—started punk zines that included poetry, diary entries, art photography, drawings, and all kinds of noodlings, doodlings, and way out scribblings.

I started my zine at the age of 13, using my bar mitzvah money to pay for the photocopying. I called it *Rag in Chains*. I gave myself the alias Shredder, because, in those days, kids used to "shred" at skateboarding the bowls at skate parks. One kid would say to another, "Yeah, dude, you were shredding in the whale bowl!"

I wanted to write about the bands that weren't getting any coverage in the major press: the Germs, Black Flag, the Circle Jerks, Fear, the Adolescents, TSOL. To interview them, I'd call up their tiny independent record companies and ask for a good time to talk to them, or I'd introduce myself to the band at concerts. Then I'd either take the bus to meet them (usually at Foster's Freeze , Schwab's, or the House of Pies) *or* I'd interview them over the phone and record them with a little suction cup microphone that I bought at Radio Shack. Before we began the interview, I always said, "By law I must let you know that I am taping you."

Soon, I got my friends at school involved. Some friends helped take pictures, some helped paste it all up, some helped collate and staple. Together, we'd write columns about ANYTHING we thought was funny or interesting: the worst shows on television, how to share a single hot fudge sundae between five people, insane beatnik poetry written on the insides of candy wrappers that made no sense, and very stupid comic strips. We passed *Rag in Chains* out at school and took it to all the local record stores. We got on mailing lists and gave copies away at punk shows. After the first issue, I started to receive about ten pieces of mail a day—some from places as far away as Italy and Norway! Sometimes we would see a complete stranger sitting on the bus, reading our zine!

Putting out a zine was like being part of a secret society that very few grown-ups knew about. Your not-so-secret mission: to tell it YOUR way *one hundred percent*.

So Easy it Amazed us!

How do they do it?

What they can do, you can do!

a Plan

A HOT TIP!

IT'S QUICK AND EASY!

Do's and Don'ts

So-o-o Tempting

The marvelous new do-it-yourself

Why Swelter?

from this

TO THIS

HERE'S ALL YOU DO:

MONEY BACK GUARANTEE

If for any reason you are not 100% delighted with your

"I just realized what I'd been missing"

SECTION TWO

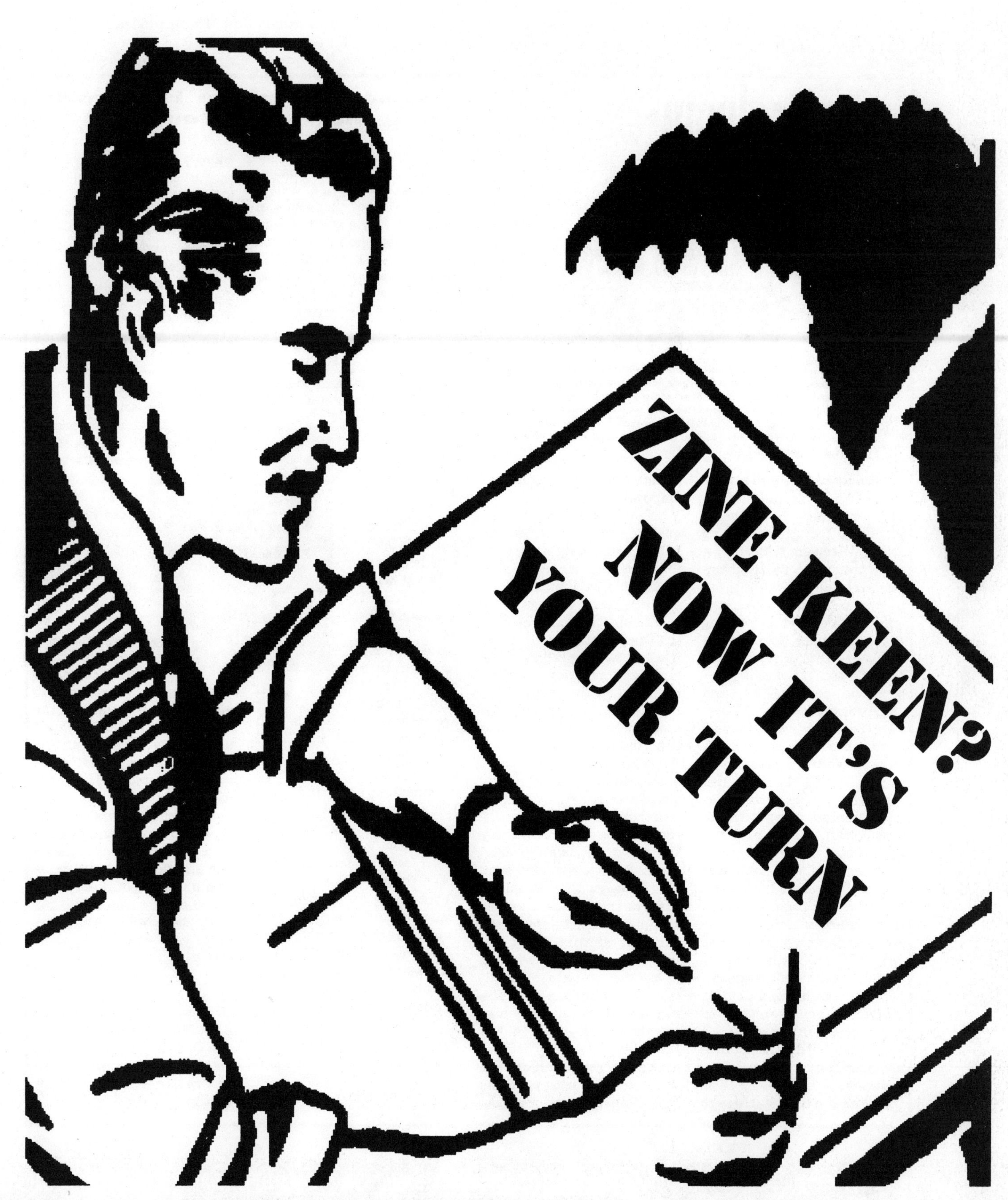

ZINE SCREAM

SPEAKING OUT THROUGH WRITING

The following excerpt, written by one of your ZINE SCENE authors and adressing the importance of self-expression, is from *Writes of Passage: A Literary Journal for Teens.*

guest column

Hillary Carlip

the POWER of your WORDS

"Sometimes paper is the only thing that will listen to you."

I started keeping journals when I was thirteen years old. Okay, I don't have to spell out exactly how many years ago that was, but let's just say I have filled almost an entire bookcase with those once-empty black books. Writing was my solace. My savior. It was the only place I could express myself fully. No matter how angry, confused, terrified, sappy, distraught, love crazed, insecure, hopeful or hopeless I felt.

Since writing has always been such a vital part of my life and survival, several years ago I started teaching creative writing workshops, as a volunteer, to disadvantaged teenagers. What I try to inspire in those I teach, as I encourage everyone reading this to consider, is that writing (along with other forms of creative self-expression) can be a tool for healing and empowerment.

From my own personal experience and, specifically, from the young women I have taught, I've found that when girls hit adolescence, they have a tendency to go inward, shut down, lose confidence and become self-conscious. However, I believe that if girls commit their thoughts to writing, they can begin to regard them as important, and realize that their own ideas are as vital in the world as anyone else's. Likewise, boys can also benefit from personal writing. It offers an opportunity to explore creativity, sensitivity and emotional depths not usually encouraged in boys. I believe that by expressing their thoughts and letting others be affected by them, teens are empowered.

With writing, you can examine your feelings and beliefs, providing a catalyst for revelation. When a feeling is internalized, it expands and can become overwhelming. As emotions are released onto paper, it often leads to healing. Writing can be a tool for transformation, shining the light on the inside, taking you through external layers and bringing you closer to your soul.

Recently, when I came across a quote from a teenage girl, I was struck by its precise truth:
"Sometimes paper is the only thing that will listen to you."

I chose to open my book *Girl Power* with that quote. *Girl Power* gives teenage girls an opportunity to speak out through writing. I got the idea for the book when I began the volunteer teaching I mentioned at a residential treatment center for "troubled" girls in Los Angeles. The majority of these girls are in gangs and/or have committed crimes; they come from long histories of abuse, abandonment, incest, drugs and alcohol. They are uncommunicative at best, and usually what does come out of their mouths is guarded and hostile. Yet when I presented the opportunity for them to be heard, to safely put on paper what they wouldn't dare say aloud, something dramatic occured. Without the fear of being laughed at, judged, or simply misunderstood, the girls came to life. I saw a side that not many people get to see: their depth, vulnerability and wisdom.

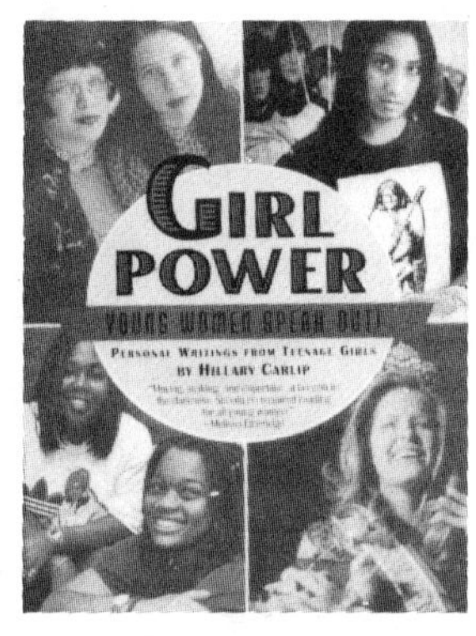

A bookcase full of journals later, I'm better at talking with people than I was as a teenager. It's easier for me to communicate and I know there are at least some people who will listen to me. But I still keep a journal. I continue to need a place to let everything out unedited, and I find when I'm in a situation where I could use a bit of enlightenment, that kind of writing often leads me to clarity.

There's also something about going back to my old journals and seeing what I was going through years ago —especially when I was a teenager. Like most young women, it was a particularly challenging time for me.

I was an insecure, overweight girl who thought I'd never find love. I was often teased about my appearance and was even given the nickname "Fanny" (comparable to Fat Ass nowadays!) The only way I could accept being an "outcast" was to make it appear like I was doing it on purpose, and with style, so I ate fire and juggled my way through high school and college. It gave me a different kind of attention.

But the name Fanny echoed through me for years and years—even when I lost weight, got in a relationship, and was no longer teased. I look back at my journals written by Fanny and I see clearly how she used writing to get through that deeply torturous time.

When my editor asked me to include a dedication in *Girl Power*, it was obvious to me who inspired the book the most—who also could have benifited so greatly if she knew just how powerful she was. I dedicated *Girl Power* to Fanny.

Every person who takes a pen to paper and speaks from within, allowing his or her emotions to surface, is committing a courageous act of self-empowerment.

Write, Write, Write. Express yourselves. Be powerful.

Hillary Carlip lives in Los Angeles, California, where she is a screenwriter and an artist. Her book, Girl Power, is available from Warner Books.

FREE EXPRESSION AND RESPONSIBILITY

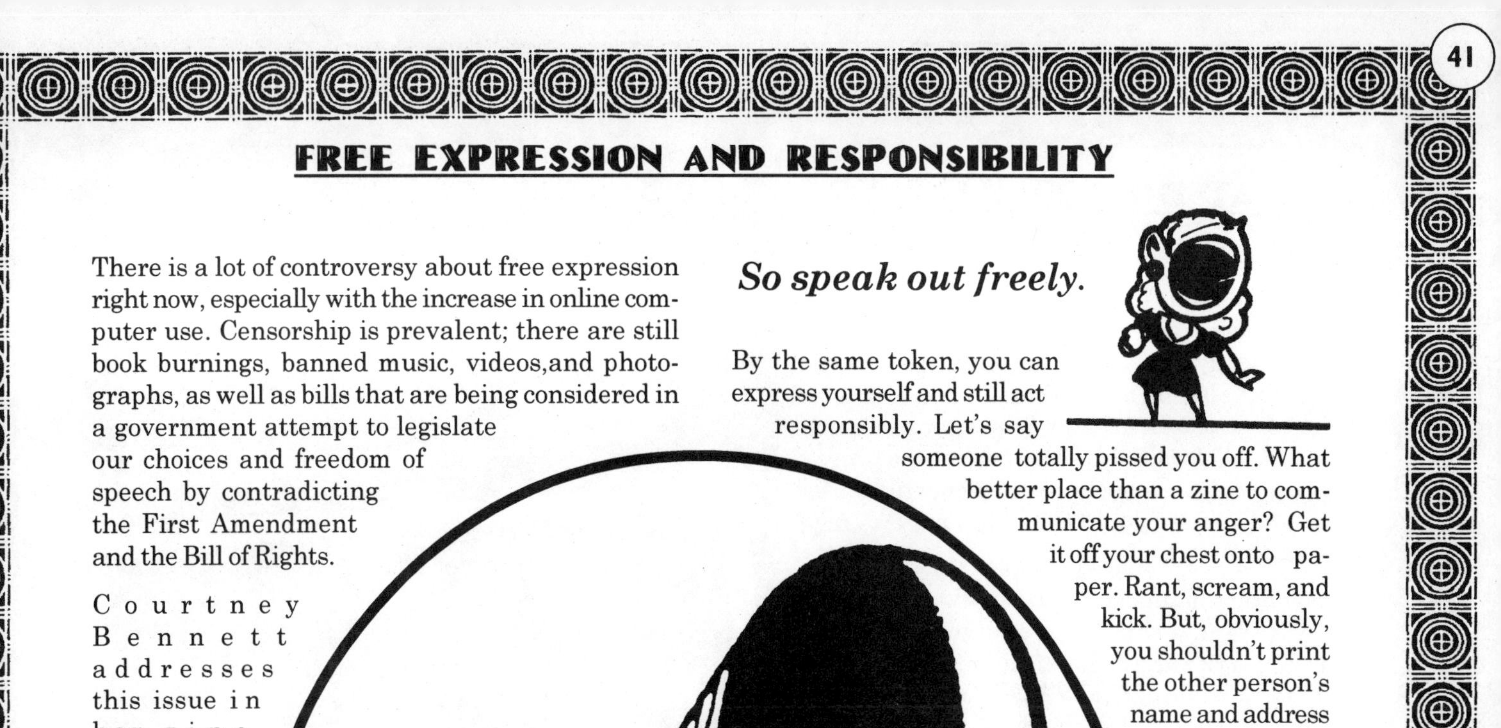

There is a lot of controversy about free expression right now, especially with the increase in online computer use. Censorship is prevalent; there are still book burnings, banned music, videos,and photographs, as well as bills that are being considered in a government attempt to legislate our choices and freedom of speech by contradicting the First Amendment and the Bill of Rights.

Courtney Bennett addresses this issue in her zine BITCHFIELD #20:

"First the Internet, then the mail . . . . we can't let this happen. If nothing else it will destroy the thinking section of the population from effectively communicating with one another. It will eventually destroy zinesters and all the people involved with zines as information. It will destroy simple things like album reviews on the net by blocking out 'inappropriate' words . . . . It could easily lead to a movement where the gov't actually polices what is sent via mail—such as in Canada/Australia where many zines/records/books have been held in customs entering the country."

Most likely we all have *enough* people in our lives telling us what we should and shouldn't, can and can't say. Zines are places to *fully* express yourself no matter how challenging or scandalous your feelings might be.

So speak out freely.

By the same token, you can express yourself and still act responsibly. Let's say someone totally pissed you off. What better place than a zine to communicate your anger? Get it off your chest onto paper. Rant, scream, and kick. But, obviously, you shouldn't print the other person's name and address or encourage people to go bomb their house or send snakes in the mail. Creating and distributing zines that are racist, classist, ageist, sexist, homophobic, etc. only promotes further hatred and intolerance. There's enough disrespect, prejudice, and bigotry in the world. Why perpetuate these things in a zine?

Of course, what free speech means is that it's your prerogative to write about anything you desire, and of course, we're all free to read or not read it. But we can only hope your zine will inspire.

Inspire readers to action, to new thought, to understanding, to feeling a bit better about themselves. Inspire others to be honest, courageous, outspoken. To get in touch with their anger, their pain, their shame, their joy. Inspire readers' imaginations, creativity, sense of awe, magic, and *power* within themselves. Inspire brilliant ideas and ordinary musings. Inspire readers to know that what they have to say *can* and *does* make a difference.

WHAT DO YOU HAVE TO SAY?

Just think about it. Once upon a time a certain sperm chose a certain egg and that turned into you. Basically you are miraculous for that event alone. But also, on a daily basis, you survive bad TV, mean teachers, grumpy bosses, broken hearts, holidays, fast food, depression, and maybe worse—AIDS, poverty, misogyny, abuse—but still you are here, and you are you. That's even more miraculous and worth celebrating.

So celebrate it zineishly—as only you can. If you are a student, a chicken fryer, a punk rawker, a riot grrrl, a riot nrrrd, flower child, faerie-believer, goddess worshiper, sk8 head, snow boarder, thrifter, music fanatic, cine-maniac, or manic depressive; if you are wild, shy, self-aggrandizing, self-effacing, a magical thinker, or a hard-core realist—express it with your zine.

You are what makes your zine one-of-a-kind and worth the read, so don't be afraid to explore all the things you really feel passionate about.

Colette, the French author, gave this advice to a young writer: "Look for a long time at what pleases you, and longer still at what pains you." It's important to write about the things in your life that hurt as well.

Ranting-on about what pains you may seem self-involved, but it could make others feel less alone, and perhaps encourage them to express themselves too.

We savor zines that show concern for the welfare of others, and suggest ways to take action: hot line numbers, resource lists, self-defense and street survival techniques, healing tips, stickers with activist slogans, loving advice, and positive words.

It's beauteous to see people using their zines as a way to send forth sparkles of light into the dark.

JANUARY 1

Last night - NEW YEAR'S EVE - Virginia came over and stayed to welcome the New Year" 1942" until 2:30 a.m. Went to bed and didn't wake til' nearly noon today. Tati had to work even today as they are very busy with defense work at Packard's Aircraft Division. We (Mami & I) loft around all afternoon. At 3:30 p.m. Trifu, my

HOW DO YOU SAY IT?

Now you know you want to create a zine. You know you have something to say but what if you've never written much of anything before except for that fourth grade report on the Boll Weevil, or the letter to your annoying aunt thanking her for the crocheted pancho she sent?

There are ever so many ways to start writing, and we're going to give you a few tips. For those of you who are already pros, you never know what could catapult you into a different direction, so read on!

STREAM OF CONSCIOUSNESS WRITING

Take pen to paper and write, WRITE, WRITE. Don't let your mind get in the way. Write whatever comes to you, whether it makes sense or not. Don't stop yourself. Don't judge what's pouring out. In fact, don't even read it or pay attention to it yet. Just let it flow without inhibition.

Another way to get into a stream of consciousplace is to talk into a tape recorder. Then you can transcribe it later. Again, just blab on. About anything. About nothing. The point is to free yourself up. Don't stop yourself by being judgmental.

DREAM ON

You spend half your life dreaming, so why not use that time to feed your conscious work? Just wake up and jot down your dreams and half-asleep ideas. Don't waste such rich, free material!

PICK AN EMOTION

You can generally begin writing by tapping into what you're feeling. You can also pick an emotion that you aren't necessarily experiencing at the time. What pisses you off beyond words? What makes you elated, confused, uppity, freaked out, blissed out, worn out? Write about it.

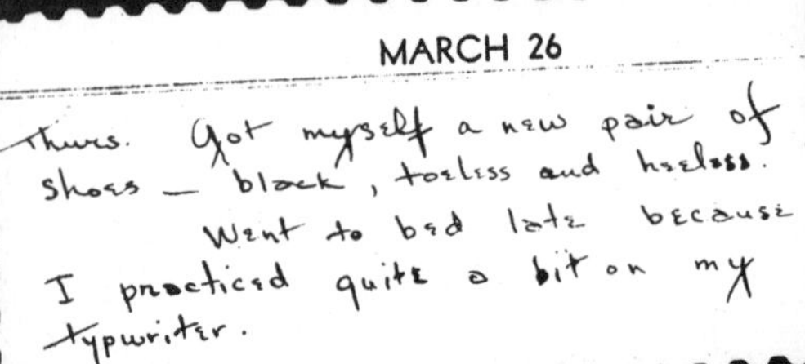

MARCH 26

Thurs. Got myself a new pair of shoes — black, toeless and heelless. Went to bed late because I practiced quite a bit on my typewriter.

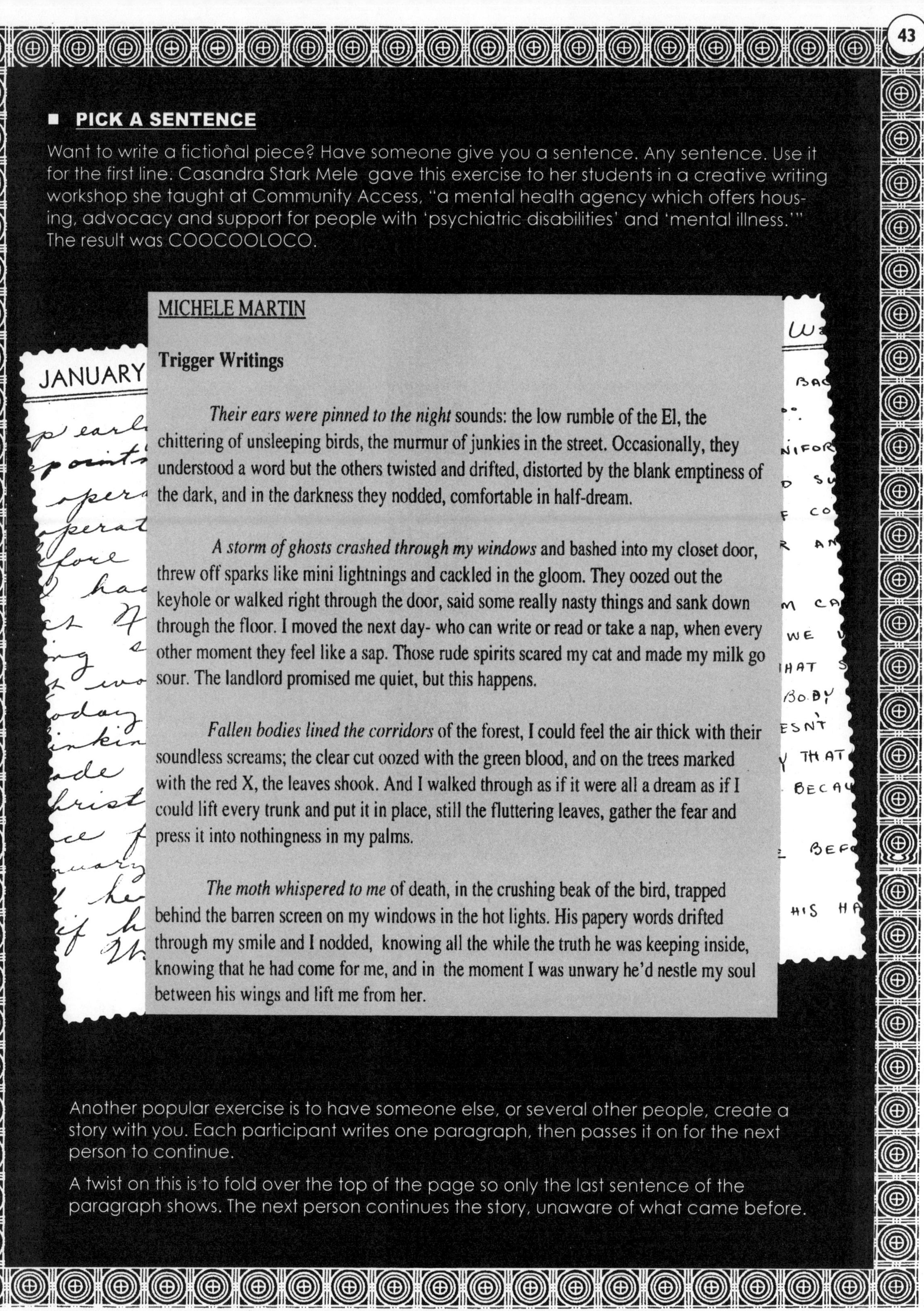

■ PICK A SENTENCE

Want to write a fictional piece? Have someone give you a sentence. Any sentence. Use it for the first line. Casandra Stark Mele gave this exercise to her students in a creative writing workshop she taught at Community Access, "a mental health agency which offers housing, advocacy and support for people with 'psychiatric disabilities' and 'mental illness.'" The result was COOCOOLOCO.

MICHELE MARTIN

Trigger Writings

Their ears were pinned to the night sounds: the low rumble of the El, the chittering of unsleeping birds, the murmur of junkies in the street. Occasionally, they understood a word but the others twisted and drifted, distorted by the blank emptiness of the dark, and in the darkness they nodded, comfortable in half-dream.

A storm of ghosts crashed through my windows and bashed into my closet door, threw off sparks like mini lightnings and cackled in the gloom. They oozed out the keyhole or walked right through the door, said some really nasty things and sank down through the floor. I moved the next day- who can write or read or take a nap, when every other moment they feel like a sap. Those rude spirits scared my cat and made my milk go sour. The landlord promised me quiet, but this happens.

Fallen bodies lined the corridors of the forest, I could feel the air thick with their soundless screams; the clear cut oozed with the green blood, and on the trees marked with the red X, the leaves shook. And I walked through as if it were all a dream as if I could lift every trunk and put it in place, still the fluttering leaves, gather the fear and press it into nothingness in my palms.

The moth whispered to me of death, in the crushing beak of the bird, trapped behind the barren screen on my windows in the hot lights. His papery words drifted through my smile and I nodded, knowing all the while the truth he was keeping inside, knowing that he had come for me, and in the moment I was unwary he'd nestle my soul between his wings and lift me from her.

Another popular exercise is to have someone else, or several other people, create a story with you. Each participant writes one paragraph, then passes it on for the next person to continue.

A twist on this is to fold over the top of the page so only the last sentence of the paragraph shows. The next person continues the story, unaware of what came before.

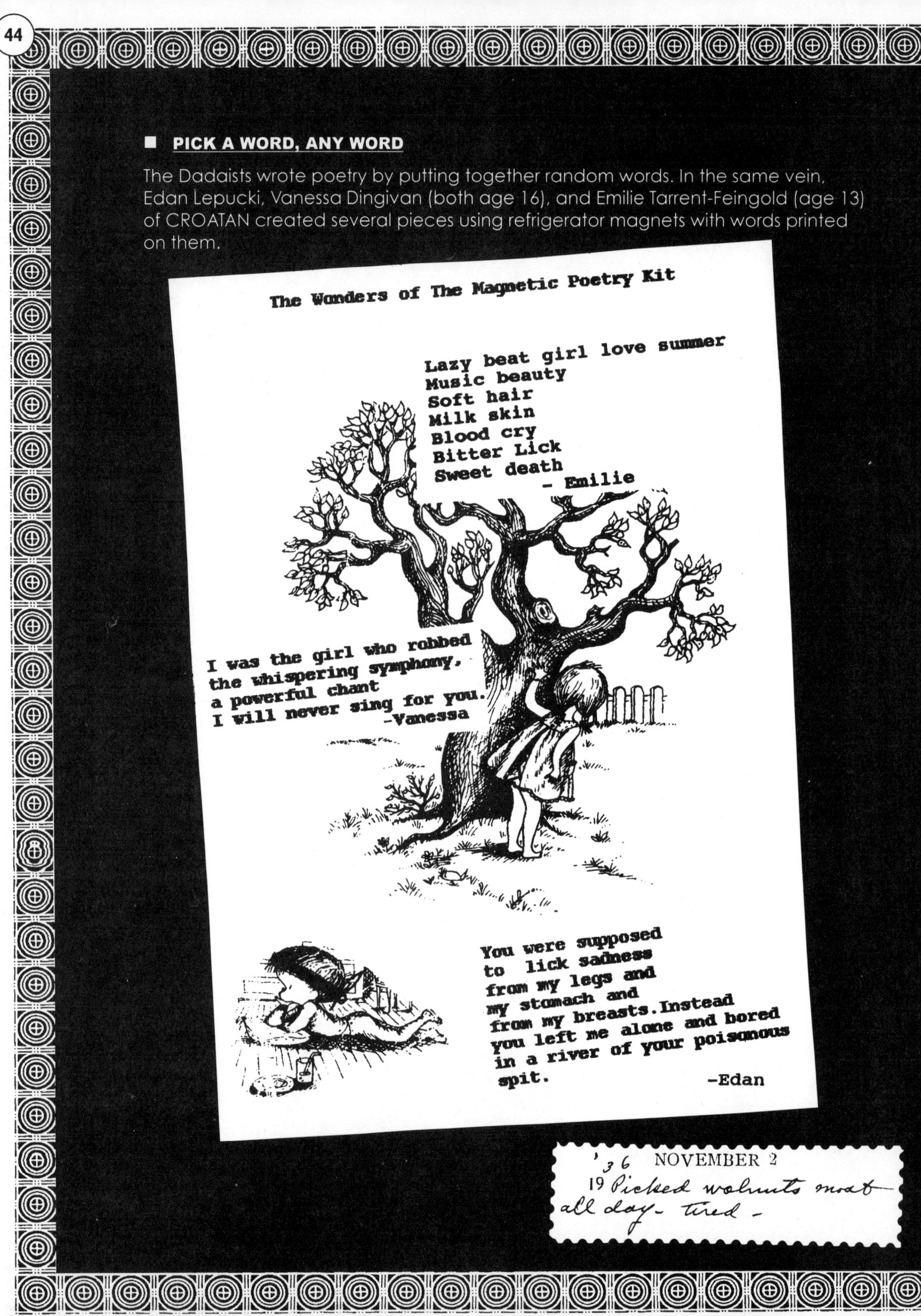

PICK A WORD, ANY WORD

The Dadaists wrote poetry by putting together random words. In the same vein, Edan Lepucki, Vanessa Dingivan (both age 16), and Emilie Tarrent-Feingold (age 13) of CROATAN created several pieces using refrigerator magnets with words printed on them.

The Wonders of The Magnetic Poetry Kit

Lazy beat girl love summer
Music beauty
Soft hair
Milk skin
Blood cry
Bitter Lick
Sweet death
- Emilie

I was the girl who robbed
the whispering symphony,
a powerful chant
I will never sing for you.
-Vanessa

You were supposed
to lick sadness
from my legs and
my stomach and
from my breasts.Instead
you left me alone and bored
in a river of your poisonous
spit.
-Edan

'36 NOVEMBER 2
19 Picked walnuts most all day - tired -

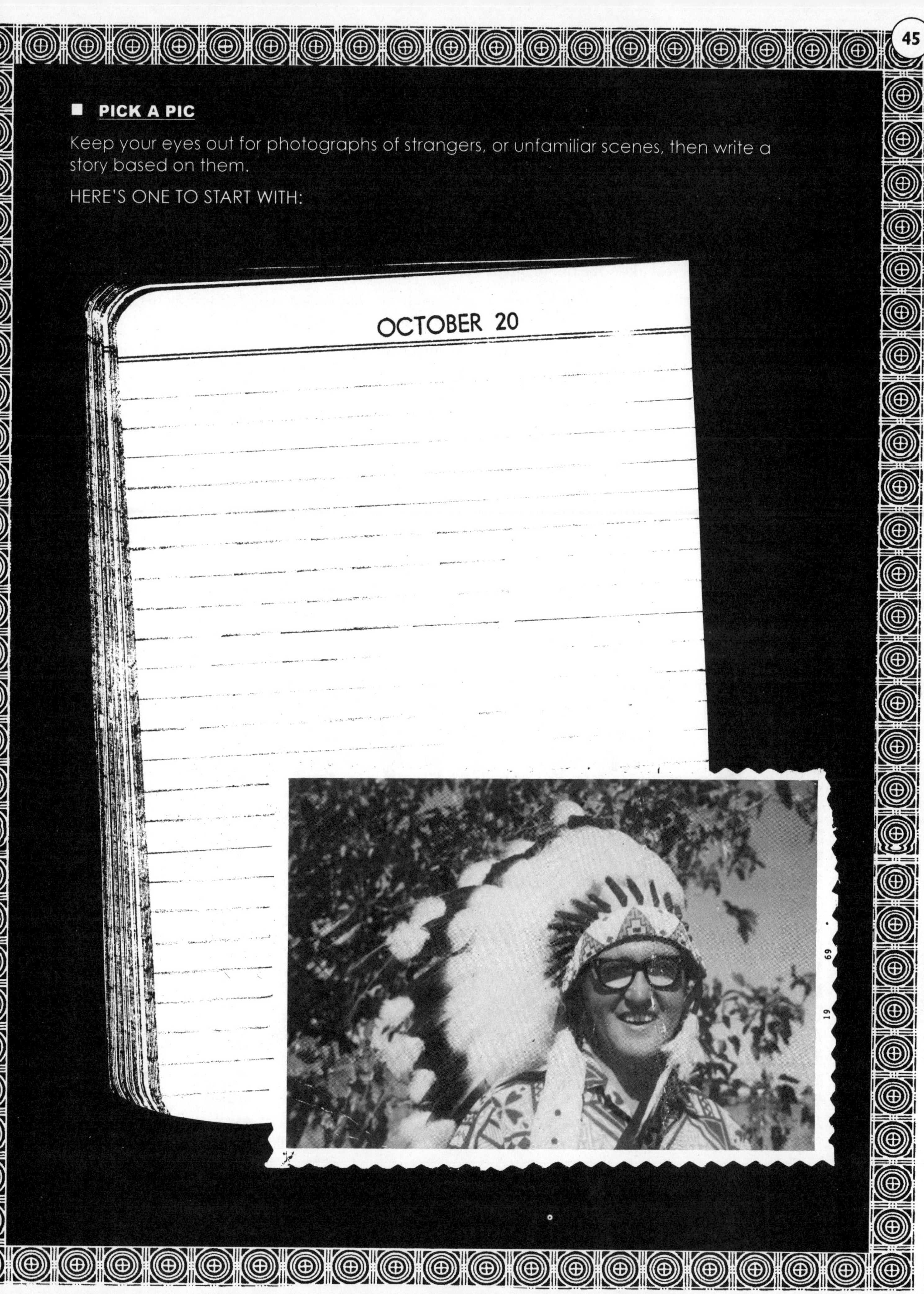

■ PICK A PIC

Keep your eyes out for photographs of strangers, or unfamiliar scenes, then write a story based on them.

HERE'S ONE TO START WITH:

DESCRIPTIVE WRITING

When choosing zines to excerpt, we were drawn to the ones that were not only soul-bearing, humorous, painful and real, but also rich with descriptive details.

The most tempting zine writing lures with a dazzle of vivid, concrete images: critters, babes, totems, doilies, robots, scary monstas, teddy bears, big shoes, sk8 demons, drag queenies, Ferris wheels, and koi fish.

A good way to make your writing more scintillating is to think about your **senses**. What do things look, sound, smell, taste, feel like? It's fun to mix them up.

For example: Describe how a color looks according to smell, or what a taste is like according to feel—i.e. the *bitter yellow; the velvety soup*; or how about the *bitter yellow velvety soup*?

Write slowly and carefully, with tender attention to every sense. Compare our lifeless example to Biz Miller's vibrant "Queen of Coney Island."

"There was a woman who did interesting things in Coney Island where she had a friend."

versus

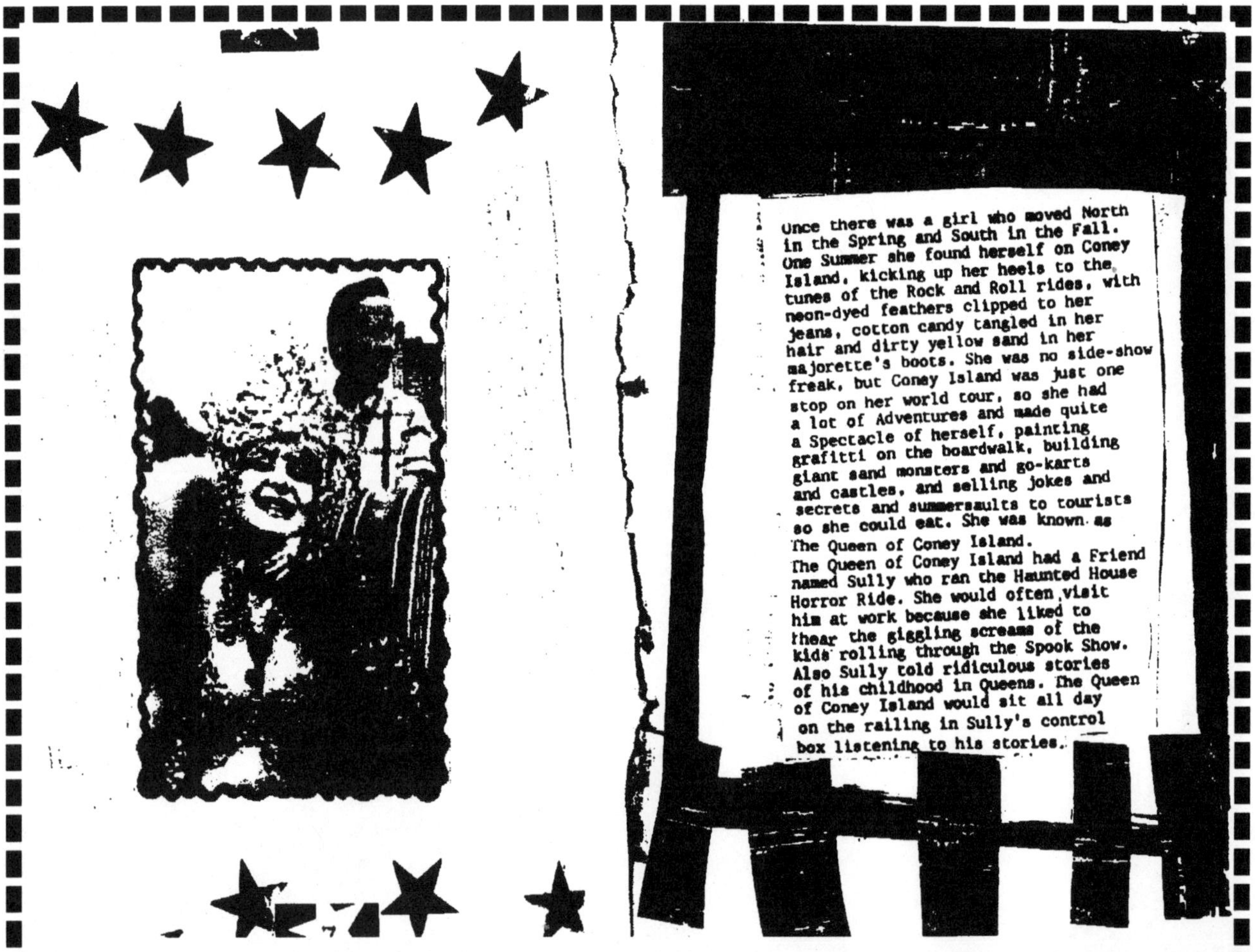

Once there was a girl who moved North in the Spring and South in the Fall. One Summer she found herself on Coney Island, kicking up her heels to the tunes of the Rock and Roll rides, with neon-dyed feathers clipped to her jeans, cotton candy tangled in her hair and dirty yellow sand in her majorette's boots. She was no side-show freak, but Coney Island was just one stop on her world tour, so she had a lot of Adventures and made quite a Spectacle of herself, painting grafitti on the boardwalk, building giant sand monsters and go-karts and castles, and selling jokes and secrets and summersaults to tourists so she could eat. She was known as The Queen of Coney Island.
The Queen of Coney Island had a Friend named Sully who ran the Haunted House Horror Ride. She would often visit him at work because she liked to hear the giggling screams of the kids rolling through the Spook Show. Also Sully told ridiculous stories of his childhood in Queens. The Queen of Coney Island would sit all day on the railing in Sully's control box listening to his stories.

Biz Miller, THE GAME #5; photo by Nancy Breslowe

Your words can paint pictures and your pictures can tell stories. You can fill your zine with imagery as wild and wonderlandish as a dream.

ZINE THEME

SOME THINGS TO INCLUDE

Hopefully by now you've gotten the idea that there is no one way to do a zine. No rules. No limitations. But there ARE certain elements that often pop up: a cover, intro, table of contents, letters, interviews, poetry, faves, rants, recipes, fashion, make yr own stuff, contests and polls, reviews, comix, per-writing, misc. things, and an outro. And even if this sounds like some sort of formula, the way *you*, as an individual, treat these particular subjects will, naturally, make them unique.

THE COVER

You could just start your zine right there on the first page, but we'd say 99.9% of the zines we've seen have covers. But don't think "Oh, how rigid." Within the world of covers, there are many places to go.

Most covers feature a photo, drawing, or a clip art (copyright-free) image, along with the title (see PICKING A NAME, page 81) and issue number. You can also include the price—if you're going to charge money for your zine.

On the cover of GIRL INFINITY #2 is a picture of the editors' friend who did a "glamour makeover" photo shoot as a joke. Using glitter pens, the eds. enhanced her bouffanted glam-shot with red sparkly lips and shiny blue eyeshadow.

Mariah McDougall hand-crafted the cover of each copy of MAGDALENE #1 from a brown paper bag. She glued photos on each bag cover and cut out letters to form the title.

There are covers that use sandpaper remnants, others with dog bones and Pez candies glued on; zines mounted inside matchbooks, and titles made by old plastic

LABEL MAKERS

You can have your cover reflect what's inside your zine, or not. Gina Young, age 17, whose PRIVATE CATHOLIC is an outlet for venting, "feelings about private/catholic/conservative schools," goes for the connection with her school notebook cover.

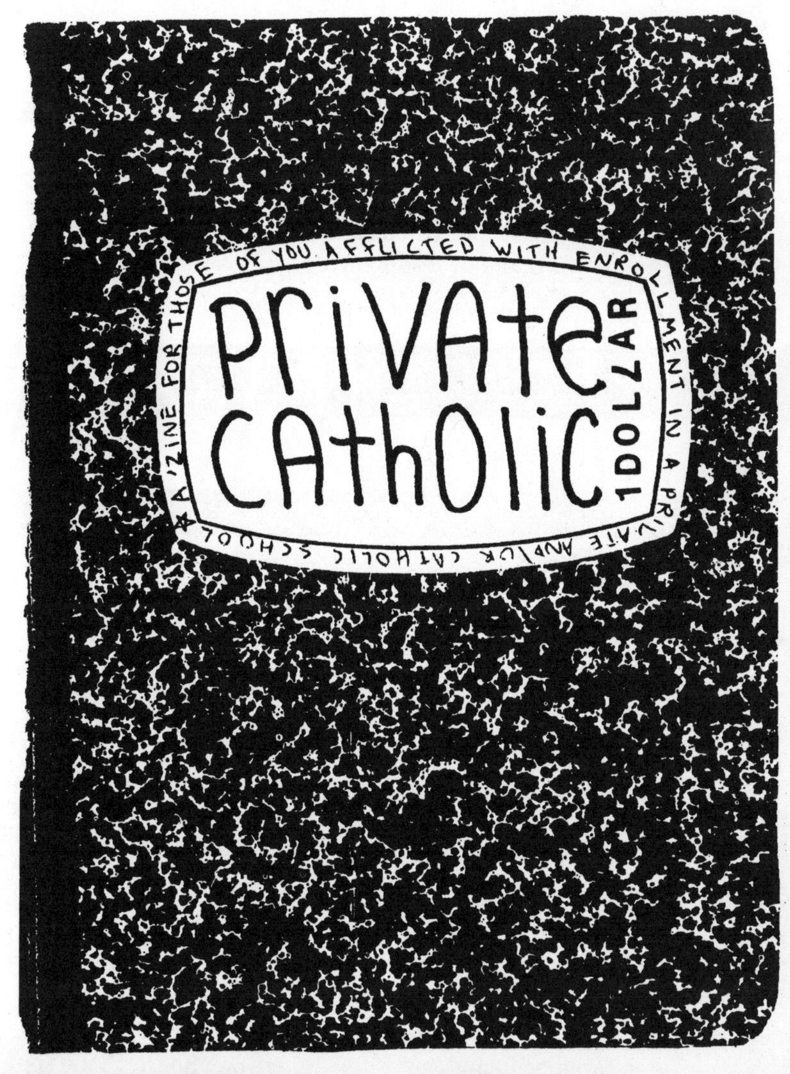

WHAT ABOUT THE BACK COVER? Many zinesters avoid the expense of envelopes by putting the receiver's address directly on the back cover of the zine along with a return address and postage. Some even frame the address box with wacky lead-ins:

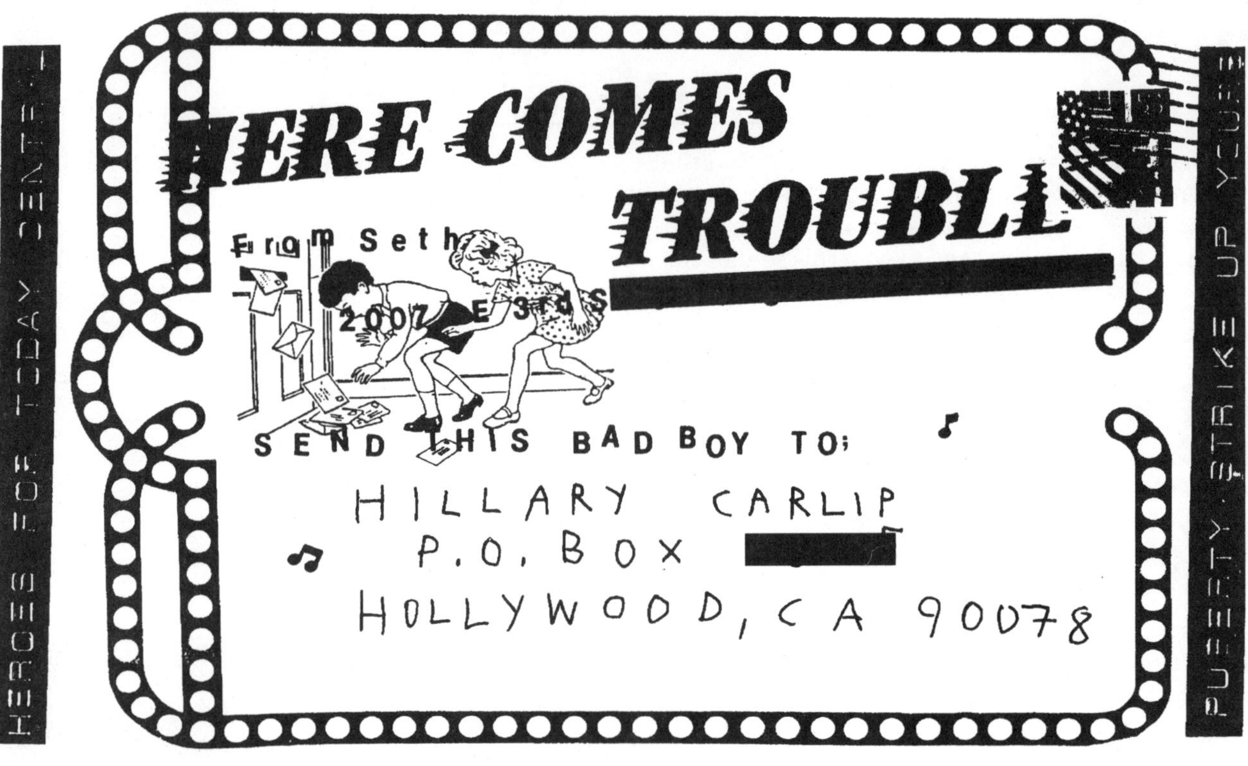

Seth Bogard, PUBERTY STRIKE

By not using an envelope, you can just tape or staple your zine shut and send it off. You can even include a personal note or letter inside.

That just about covers covers! ONWARD TO:

INTROS

On the inside cover of a zine, you'll usually find an introduction.

An intro can simply be a greeting, but some zinesters use it as a place to apologize for how long it took them to get the issue out. We don't think this is necessary since doing a zine is not really about meeting deadlines—unless you have a list of paid subscribers awaiting your next issue.

Your intro can also include an overview of what's inside, or that can be left to a table of contents (or not done at all). Mostly, it's a place to share information about yourself and your zine.

We found that the intros that most captured our attention were ones that really looked and sounded like the person who was writing them. In other words, be yourself. That individuality is what makes the whole zine revolution alive. You could even use a photo or a drawing of yourself to give your reader an image of who they'll be spending the next bit of time with.

Some zinesters, who've been courageous enough to spill their guts and pass them around, aren't necessarily willing to use their real names. An alias is always an option. But others are identifying themselves loud and proud, like THE FLABBY ARM's Molly Aviva Brodak, age 16, who writes:

"I don't use an alias because I promised myself I wouldn't be embarrassed by anything I print, so this holds me to my vow."

Don't give away too much in your intro. Leave something for the zine itself. Try not to say too little, either. You don't want to bore your reader—they may not want to read any further. Be fairly brief, to the point, funny if you're so inclined, informative, and vivid. Go for words that you really use in life. Made-up words can also help to *slinktrifically* expand your readers' vocabularies.

Make your reader feel like they're very, very lucky to be here with you, about to embark on a journey into the lush landscape of your head and heart: your zine!

You may want to try to convey the passionate reason why you couldn't help starting this zine in the first place. If you're convincing, your reader will want to check out your zine for the same reasons you wanted to write it.

Here's what Mariah McDougall (MAGDALENE and REWM) says:

"i was hypnotized by this stuff clawing at my hands, telling them to createcreatecreate and tell * so i did cos... my heart is who wears the pants in this gurl... i'm doing just what i'm told."

I hate introductions - I would make my zine introduction-less, but then it wouldn't feel right. Most people put some sorta mundane but interesting fact about their life here. My entire zine is a projection, a diary, of my life and mind - it is my introduction. But maybe the official introduction should be an intro to myself as a whole - whereas my zine is an introduction to detailed parts of my existence. But if I tell you just straight facts will you prejudge me then?? Will you form yr opinion before reading what I really am as opposed to who I appear to be? You would do it if you met me face to face - would you do it now? Zines give their authors anonymity - one can read a zine and never know the author's appearance, age, even their sexual preference. They must base their judgment on the meat of the author's writings - and nothing superficial. By stating plain facts about myself I am risking you closing yr mind on me before you get beyond this official introduction. But in telling you these things I am also given a chance to prove yr prejudices wrong.

So I will give you an introduction to the basic and whole Melissa. I am an 18 year old high-school dropout currently getting her G.E.D.. I am slightly overweight and definitely short (5'3 1/2"). I have pale skin with some freckles and auburn hair. I am bisexual. I am descended from Native Americans (Lakota), Irish, German, Scottish, and a few more. (a true genetic mutt) If you met me on the street you'd see a woman with above shoulder length hair pinned back by baby barrettes & my eyes are Indian eyes (often called Oriental by mistake). I would most likely be wearing a t-shirt, sweat jacket, jeans, strange shoes, & cat's eye sunglasses.

Now that you have an image of me with all the prejudices that come with this image, I'd like to let you see the "real" deeper me.

Hope you like this zine or that it at least makes you think - I'd rather you think then like me anyways.

Love & Madness,
Melissa

Melissa Albach, LOOKING GLASS GIRL #2

TABLE OF CONTENTS

You may choose to plunge right into your zine or give your reader a clue to what's up ahead with a tantalizing preview like Elizabeth, age 16, does in SHERA (FREEDOM SLUT)#4.

LETTERS

Some zines are made up only of correspondence such as BOOK OF LETTERS, Richard's mail to Public Relations Departments and their responses. Others just publish a few real or fictional letters written by their readers. If you're reading an outrageous Seth Bee zine, you may not be able to figure out what's real and what's not.

Dear Editor

Now I don't want to bore you all to hell with all the crappy mail I get about Applebee's, so I have narrowed down the mail section to my favorite letters. And then I have even further narrowed it down to my favorite parts of the letters. And to start things off, here is the entire letter I got from Applebee's headquarters International.

Dear Seth,
How do you reward the all-time Applebee's #1 chicken finger fan? The simple answer is that I am not quite sure yet. However, I do ask that you accept the Applebee's stuff in the box as a bribe to continue sending me copies of the "zine". It is really starting to get a lot of play around the office here. So much we had to introduce a "closed door" policy in the offices while reading the "zine". It seems that nobody was getting anything done because they were constantly asking each other what they were laughing at, and then they would want to read the "zine" together. We don't mind though, because we think it is great there is someone else out there who loves Applebee's as much as we do.
If it is possible, I think it would be cool if you could send me 4 or 5 "Box Sets" of your issues so far. I want to pass them around to some of the big wigs here at the home office (it seems the "zine" makes it to the secretary level, then goes to another secretary and never gets to the bad boys who sign the pay checks around here). I think they would enjoy reading them. Enclosed is some $$$ to make the task easier. Please also send a copy to the guy who heads up the Arizona franchise. He's the BIG MAN down in the AZ market and probably the guy who will want to have "Applebee's #1 fan day". Don't fret, though because I hear you get to kiss some Applebabe's, just like the race car drivers do when they give you the rubber chicken trophy. Oh yea, he is also the guy to talk to about employment opportunities in the Tucson area.

Edward Gleich
Applebee's International, Inc.

P.S. The gift certificate is for you Birthday. My boss, Ron Marks (a big-time "Applezine" fan) wanted you to have it so you can celebrate in style at Applebee's.

Hey Edward, Thanks for the bribes and everything but I'm no sell-out! Just kidding, I'll be waiting for the day when an evelope arrives in my mail box with un-limited Applebee's gift certificates. Oh how nice "celebrate in style." I live with my folks, they paid for my birthday dinner at Applebee's. But come on, all this hard work and I still have to pay for my food!

Dear Cheth,
Family restaurants are satan's tool. Apparently you have a real problem. I do not relate. Nonetheless, you are witty. I thank Jesus I am not named after an Eric Clapton song, like Layla, and Cokie (Cocaine) Roberts are. I'm also glad my name doesn't rhyme with "Meth-breath" or "chicken death" People named Seth are weird, I think that's pretty inevitable. By the way, I'm vegetarian. Meat production/consumption as we know it has nothing to do with the healthy predator/prey relationship. It's pure, unnecessary, cruelty and waste. It's only funny/acceptable/no big deal when you don't face the reality of it.

Nick
Austin, TX

Hey now, someone needs to take a chill pill (let's go back to the 3rd grade.)
My name also rhymes with "Bad Breath" (you know, as in the 2nd series Garbage Pail Kid "Bad Breath Seth.") I'm glad my name doesn't ryhme with "penis," or " Texan-hick." I'm the predator that's right. It's not like I'm butchering little children by the thousands in my parent's house or anything.

Dearest Seth,
I think your Applebee's zine is really cool. I laughed real hard in some places. Let me cite if I may my friend Seth: one; the Darth Vadar Vs. Boba Fett "Hand over those chicken baskets..." Seeing that Boba said like three lines in his whole career it makes me crack up...oh I'm ok I didn't really crack..laugh-jeez I'm sorry. I laughed. Two: the comic is AWESOME I wish I had a childlike style (no dissing meant) and could write simple, beautiful stuff like that...sniff. Three: the Applebee's Undercover- I quote "Is it just me or does everyone pretend they have a Texan accent when they are talking to cowboys" I have that same problem Seth, but it's with the British, yknow, h'ullo mate, 'ow is your mum tewdey." Four: I guessed correctly that you were the person who eats the most chicken baskets (see #4) but I wasn't sure cause with all those famous faces I assumed you were a famous guy, but I couldn't remember where I had seen you. hmmm.... Top Gun, Goonies, Star Wars, Home Alone....

Russel
Houston, TX

Well actually, I am a famous star. But it's all a secret right now.

Seth Bogard, Boy Tycoon:
Well you've done it again. Enclosed find $32.00 for postage or whatever since Ms. Momma has locked up her stamps, how unwilling. If there is anything left to say about finger licking good ficken chingers it'll probably involve dipping, i.e. in mustard, in horse raddish, in jalepeno salsa what else. Keep up the great work.

Joe M. Davis along with
Mary H.C. Davis
Somewhere in Kentucky

Seth Bogard, APPLEBEE'S #5

INTERVIEWS

Veronica Lake, Sarah McLachlan, Pippi Longstocking, James Dean, Dr. Seuss, Gabriel García Márquez, Indigo Girls, Frida Kahlo, Marc Chagall—these are a few of the people we'd like to interview if we had the opportunity (or if the deceased ones were still alive). You might not have access to your dream interviewee, but you'd be surprised at how many people will respond to your requests for information about them and their work. Pursue anyone who sparks your interest, even if they're not radly famous.

Here are some tips on the process once you've got someone in your clutches.

HOW TO INTERVIEW

1. Talk about candy . . .

. . .or politics or books or sex or music or lunch or shoes or imaginary childhood friends or travel or pets or anything that doesn't have to do with what the person you're interviewing is mainly into. (CAKE devoted an issue to the favorite candies of various bands). You get to know a lot more about someone by focusing on unusual details rather than on what everyone always asks them about. Besides, people have probably heard all that other stuff already.

2. Storyize.

You can just print a transcript of the interview. But for a really vibrant reading experience, why not describe what the person looks, sounds, and smells like (if you get that close), just the way you would describe a character in a story? Notice details that give you and your readers clues into who this person really is. If you're doing it by mail, then ask for photos and pay attention to handwriting.

ZiNE mANIA!

ZINE MANIA! INTERVIEW QUESTIONS

Your name Serra Rose Sewitch (pronounced Seawitch)

Any zine alias? Nope

Name of your zine Moon Fuzz

How old are you? 14

How long have you been doing your zine? Since I was 13. I have 4 issu

What made you start? My mom has one. She gave me the idea.

How'd you decide what to write about/include? I mostly just searched through my piles of writing and junk

How do you distribute your zine, who reads it? Other zinesters or people who read about it in Factsheet 5

How many issues of your zine have you done? 4

How'd you pick the name? I was going to have a zine alias - Moon Fuzz - but then I just made it the title

~~How are you able to pay for your zine? From the zine sales and my Mom~~

Name 3 of your fave zines and describe 'em Suburbia - Funny, interesting, cool visuals →

What inspires you? Myself

Do you have co-writers or contributors? How'd you connect? My best friend has something to contribute to every issue

What's are your obesssions? Food and sleep and writing

Any hobbies? What are they? Drawing, writing, guitar, reading, phone.

What advice would you give to someone starting their own zine? Dig inside yourself and barf it out on paper

What's important for you to say/express in your zine? I need people to know my depressed/scared side

What's the oddest thing that's happened to you around your zine? Getting a chance to be in a book about zines

What's the coolest thing that's happened to you around your zine? I meet fantastic people! I have amazing pen pals!

Where do you work on your zine? In my room

What do you get from doing it? Self satisfaction

Francesca Lia Block
Hillary Carlip

PHONE/FAX

If you interview by phone, listen for voice nuances. You may be able to tape the conversation with your answering machine or, as Shredder mentioned in his "Things I Have Zine" piece (on page 37), you can purchase a telephone device that lets you record. Ask for permission to tape someone before you do.

And remember what your mother always told you: Beware of strangers, meet in a public place, and don't take any candy.

Serra Sewitch

3. Have the tools.

When Francesca was interviewing Tori Amos for *Spin* Magazine, her tape recorder kept acting up. Luckily Tori was very nice and patient and even helped fix it. But Francesca was pretty embarrassed. The funny thing was, half of the interview ended up recorded on high speed and Tori, who is really into faeries and talked a lot about them, sounded just like one on the tape!

4. Get the scoop without being a poop.

Your readers will inevitably want the dirt, and it's your job to get as much as possible without overstepping certain boundaries. Most people you interview will be aware of the dirt factor and probably try to give you at least a few juicy details about their personal life. But don't push them if they're not into it. Sometimes you can drop a few hints without hurting anyone, though.

5. Research.

Try to get as much info about your subject beforehand. This will make you feel more confident and help you gain their trust. They'll be flattered if you can quote lines from their songs, or passages from their books, for instance, or if you can make references to previous interviews they've done.

6. Let them know about you.

Some people won't really care that much, but for others, this can help make the interview a more positive exchange. If you have earlier issues of your zines, send them along with your interview request. If not, just write a great cover letter, briefly describing who you are and the very specific reasons why you MUST have them. (In your zine, that is!)

MY INTERVIEW WITH JEANETTE ()F The Chubbies

ME: So who's in your band? (I saw on the back of the 7" it's all you! how do you play a show with 4 instruments??)

JEANETTE: good question. When sympathy signed me, my band had broke up. Well, actually, I wanted all girls, but I hadn't found any, so i just did it myself. But now I have an all-girl band. My dream! Kelly on bass and Christine on drums. We've been together about 8 months.

ME: cool. how did you hook up with sympathy?

JEANETTE: well, long gone john, the owner, heard my demo, the seven inch you have and called me right away and asked me if I wanted to do a single? I said yes, and a full length. He said I could do a record a month if I wanted to, so I said great, let's do it.

ME: how many 7"'s do you have out?

JEANETTE: three seven inches, one cd. Oh and we're on the christmas comp for sympathy called Happy b'day baby jesus.

ME: what do the chubbies do on a normal day?

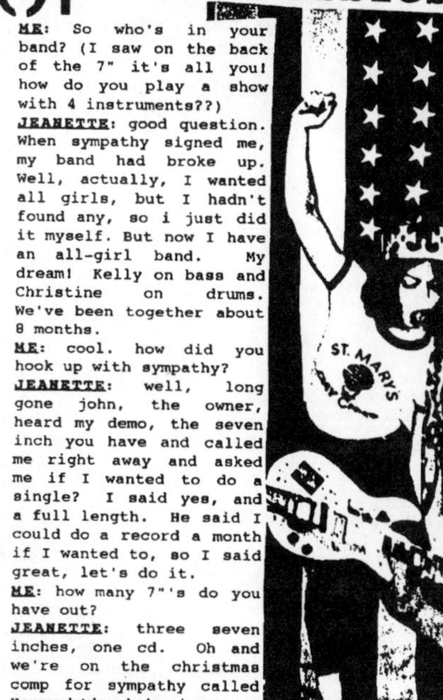

JEANETTE: unfortunately, we work. We have day jobs. Christine and Kelly are waitresses and I cut hair.
We practice a few times a week and record and tour the rest of the time.

ME: What town are you all from?

JEANETTE: I'm from Upland Ca, and Kelly's from Oceanside. That's where I live now. And Christine's from Long Beach, CA.

ME: So you're all southern california people huh? how's the smog?

JEANETTE: the smog's as dense as the inhabitants.

ME: I have friends who live down there, it seems that the whole place is like the set of Over the Edge, have you seen that movie?

JEANETTE: No, and I thought I had seen every movie ever made. Is it about cheesy, self-centered, egotistical, selfish, lazy assholes?

Excerpt from piece by Ceci, SUBURBIA #5

POETRY

Some zinesters rant about how they dislike poetry. Of all things! Little harmless, defenseless poetry. What a thing to pick on when there are problems such as violence and poverty and abuse in the world. But poetry doesn't have to be small and meek. It can be an earthquake, an avalanche, a cyclone of power. It can break you, shake you, resurrect longing, shine like an emerald city, wail like a lost ghost soul, smell like bonfires or lightning, taste like pomegranate seeds, saffron rice, fruit juice-sweetened cherry pie, feel like your lovemate's curls twining in your fingers as you tug their mouth to yours, or like the surge of a wave under your board.

However, poetry doesn't always work. Usually that's because it's not coming from a true place. What do we mean by "true place"? There's no way to really describe it. It's just a feeling and if you really tune in and listen, you'll know. It's the thing you have to express, or it will explode you into bits. A replica of your heart—it's *that* juicy and red and full of complex parts.

Let's say you want to write a poem, and you're not sure why, or where it's coming from. That's okay. No one has to read it if they don't like it. But, if you care, we think there are a few things that can make a poem stronger, and maybe less subject to rant-attack.

The first is something we've already harped on: *descriptive imagery*. We think imagery is more essential in poetry than anywhere else because of the generally short, compact nature of a poem. Each word can have significance and purpose, and can affect one or more of the senses.

Next is *rhythm*. Everything in the universe has a beat: your heart, the tide, rain, love, pain. Let your poem reflect those rhythms with quick-paced-short-staccato-tick-tocks, or languid, mellifluous, voluminous rivulets.

Also, poetry works well when it's not just images and sounds, but when the images and sounds express deep human feeling that is both universal and personal. When you write anything, especially a poem, choose a topic that has resonance for you and delve deeply into the way it makes your whole body respond. Find images and rhythms to demonstrate this.

A poem is like a human being. The descriptive language could be thought of as the body. The rhythm is like the heart. What the poem expresses is the mind. Sometimes, if it comes from that true place, poetry can even have a soul.

All of these suggestions can be applied to prose as well. The main thing is write that piece to satisfy yourself. Don't be intimidated by people who are anti-poetry. But you could also consider finding ways to slam back with something so deeply felt and gorgeously crafted that the disillusioned just might change their minds!

Here are some weapons in the poetry arsenal:

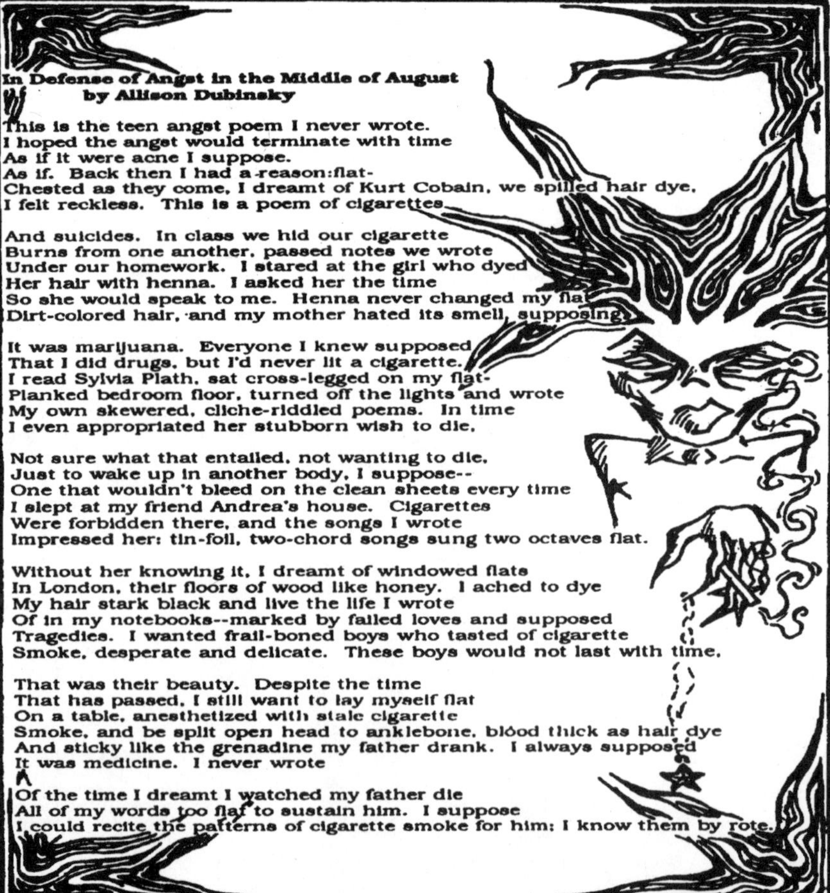

In Defense of Angst in the Middle of August
by Allison Dubinsky

This is the teen angst poem I never wrote.
I hoped the angst would terminate with time
As if it were acne I suppose.
As if. Back then I had a reason:flat-
Chested as they come, I dreamt of Kurt Cobain, we spilled hair dye,
I felt reckless. This is a poem of cigarettes

And suicides. In class we hid our cigarette
Burns from one another, passed notes we wrote
Under our homework. I stared at the girl who dyed
Her hair with henna. I asked her the time
So she would speak to me. Henna never changed my flat
Dirt-colored hair, and my mother hated its smell, supposing

It was marijuana. Everyone I knew supposed
That I did drugs, but I'd never lit a cigarette.
I read Sylvia Plath, sat cross-legged on my flat-
Planked bedroom floor, turned off the lights and wrote
My own skewered, cliche-riddled poems. In time
I even appropriated her stubborn wish to die,

Not sure what that entailed, not wanting to die,
Just to wake up in another body, I suppose--
One that wouldn't bleed on the clean sheets every time
I slept at my friend Andrea's house. Cigarettes
Were forbidden there, and the songs I wrote
Impressed her: tin-foil, two-chord songs sung two octaves flat.

Without her knowing it, I dreamt of windowed flats
In London, their floors of wood like honey. I ached to dye
My hair stark black and live the life I wrote
Of in my notebooks--marked by failed loves and supposed
Tragedies. I wanted frail-boned boys who tasted of cigarette
Smoke, desperate and delicate. These boys would not last with time.

That was their beauty. Despite the time
That has passed, I still want to lay myself flat
On a table, anesthetized with stale cigarette
Smoke, and be split open head to anklebone, blood thick as hair dye
And sticky like the grenadine my father drank. I always supposed
It was medicine. I never wrote

Of the time I dreamt I watched my father die
All of my words too flat to sustain him. I suppose
I could recite the patterns of cigarette smoke for him; I know them by rote.

from PRIVATE CATHOLIC #1

HANGOVER

Racism is the gift that keeps on giving.
I grew up in los angeles, california
but my.mind and emotions were stuck
somewhere in Europe in the past
and when I could've been sk8ting
I was brooding in the shadows,
feeling fears of busted down doors
and eyes watching in the dark.
When I was eight years old
every night I hid under the covers
imagining a gruesome parade
of lost souls marching past my bed,
if they heard me breathe or saw me
move the slightest they would take me.
It took a long time for me to look back
and see those were my aunts and uncles,
sixteen of them, and more cousins,
and their neighbors and strangers
echoing from the past before I was born.
Scientists say Holocaust survivors,
their children and grandchildren,
are biologically c anged.
We lack a chem cal that suppresses stress.
We are always waiting for that loud knock
and the kicked down door.

Ronnie Hogart, ERACISM #1

Ronnie

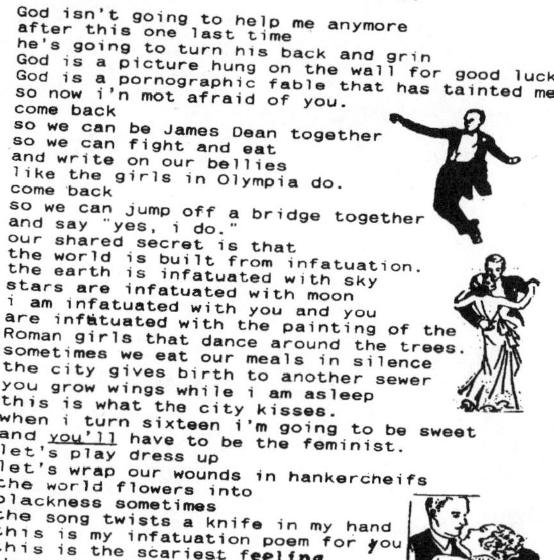

<u>Infatuation Poem</u> 7-13-94

God isn't going to help me anymore
after this one last time
he's going to turn his back and grin
God is a picture hung on the wall for good luck
God is a pornographic fable that has tainted me
so now i'n mot afraid of you.
come back
so we can be James Dean together
so we can fight and eat
and write on our bellies
like the girls in Olympia do.
come back
so we can jump off a bridge together
and say "yes, i do."
our shared secret is that
the world is built from infatuation.
the earth is infatuated with sky
stars are infatuated with moon
i am infatuated with you and you
are infatuated with the painting of the
Roman girls that dance around the trees.
sometimes we eat our meals in silence
the city gives birth to another sewer
you grow wings while i am asleep
this is what the city kisses.
when i turn sixteen i'm going to be sweet
and <u>you'll</u> have to be the feminist.
let's play dress up
let's wrap our wounds in hankercheifs
the world flowers into
blackness sometimes
the song twists a knife in my hand
this is my infatuation poem for you
this is the scariest feeling
oh god.
come back
so we can throw stones at little kids
so we can throw up coconut juice
and wind down a fireman's pole
into the core of infinite toys.
come back here

to where everything is cotton candy
i look at the christmas lights and
think of your pretty neck
i think of the monkeys that wear hats and dance
i think about all the weddings and all the
white veils
in <u>this world</u>.
i think about all the prom corsages
people keep in their refrigerators
until finally they are eaten
teenage girls devour their
teenage dreams.

Robin Crane, SWEETHEART #5

FAVE THINGS LISTS

There are very few guidelines when you're listing the things that rock your world. Just let it all out. Don't be shy. Be specific. Have fun.

THINGS WE LOVE:

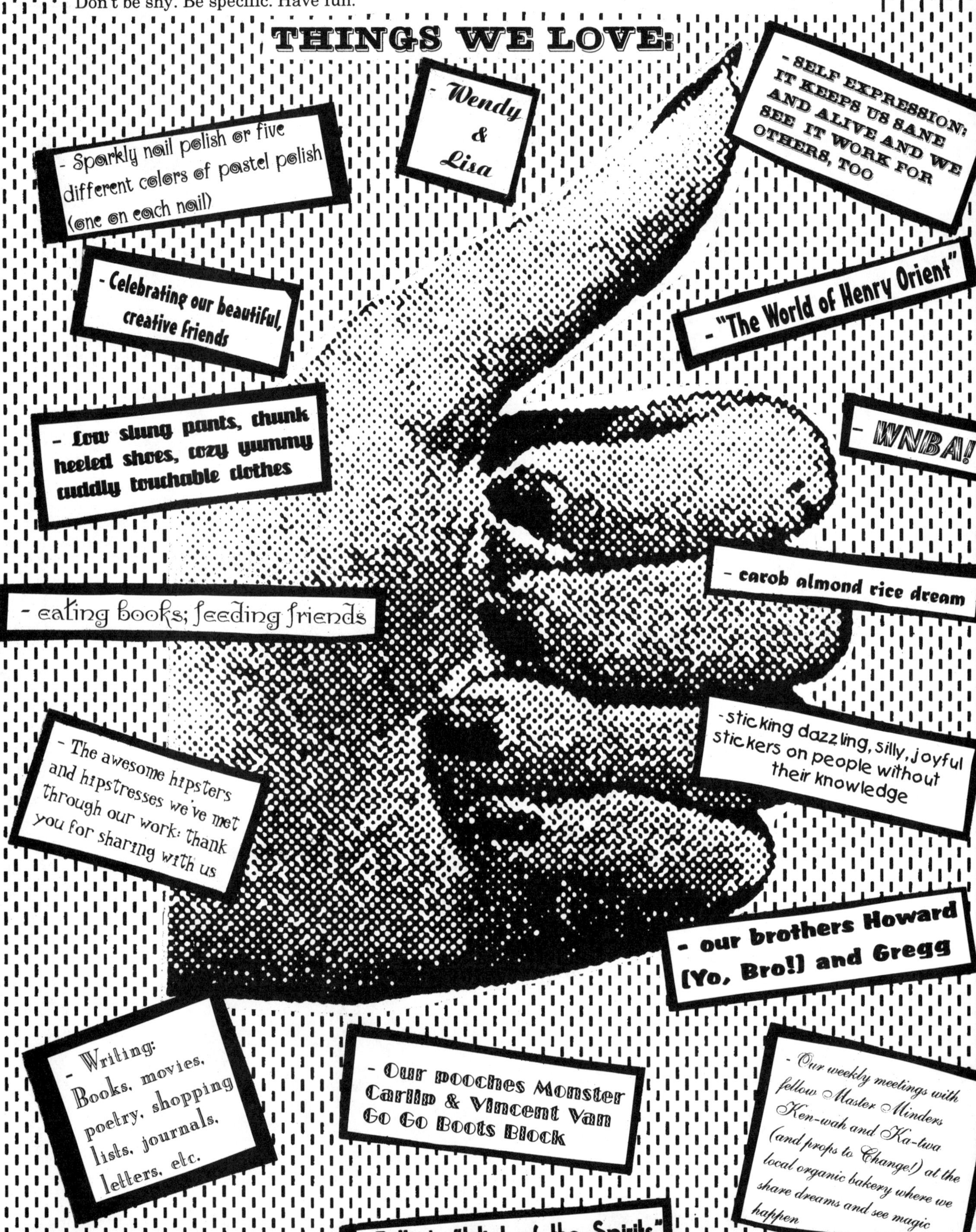

- Wendy & Lisa
- SELF EXPRESSION: IT KEEPS US SANE AND ALIVE AND WE SEE IT WORK FOR OTHERS, TOO
- Sparkly nail polish or five different colors of pastel polish (one on each nail)
- Celebrating our beautiful, creative friends
- "The World of Henry Orient"
- Low slung pants, chunk heeled shoes, cozy yummy cuddly touchable clothes
- WNBA!
- carob almond rice dream
- eating books; feeding friends
- sticking dazzling, silly, joyful stickers on people without their knowledge
- The awesome hipsters and hipstresses we've met through our work: thank you for sharing with us
- our brothers Howard [Yo, Bro!] and Gregg
- Writing: Books, movies, poetry, shopping lists, journals, letters, etc.
- Our pooches Monster Carlip & Vincent Van Go Go Boots Block
- Our weekly meetings with fellow Master Minders Ken-wah and Ka-twa (and props to Change!) at the local organic bakery where we share dreams and see magic happen
- Fellini's "Juliet of the Spirits"

tania's favorite things

- ★ supermarket fantasy by screeching weasel
- ★ ska
- ★ my black and white uniform dress
- ★ ice blended vanillas with whipped cream
- ★ my spiderman bookbag
- ★ SARA AND LIZ
- ★ MY BABY BLUE CARDIGAN
- ★ trainspotting, labrynth, the never ending story, and the
- ★ breakfast club
- ★ reel big fish
- ★ blue
- ★ greek salad
- ★ westwood
- ★ my car pippa and leopard print car seat covers
- ★ glitter
- ★ stars
- ★ cometbus and clunker
- ★ fred astaire and ginger rogers
- ★ cacao
- ★ dodge darts
- ★ pinhead gunpowder
- ★ email
- ★ pilot pens
- ★ rhinestone jewelry

A zine to crush on. Tania Rudy waxes poetic on selling popcorn, found photos, Jamaica Kincaid, and punk rock dream boys with pink hair.

These are some more of Layla Rose Cooper's (DIORAMA) favorite things:

"Go-go boots, miniskirts, '50s french novels, John Waters movies, '60s dance records, leopard prints, Japanese food from Tokyo Bowl, Indian food, Milkshakes, pets, mod!, gorgeous underwear, parties, crying and tragedies, playing hostess for my friends, old pinups/starlets/ movies, rock and roll records, drums and old organs, and research books and office supplies. I am also obsessed with drug stores, discount dept. stores, pens, blue corduroys, girlie magazines, and food."

Mmmm. Seth and I both love snacks. Here's what we like to fill our bellies

Layla . . .	Seth . . .
Ginger Ale	Rice with milk and sugar
Eggs and Toast	Root Beer floats
Potatoes	Black Bean Burritos
Chocolate Milkshakes	Tums
Carrots	V-8
Green Apples and Bananas	Jordan Almonds
Campbell's Vegetable Beef Soup	Chicken Fingers
Chicken Fingers	Tabouli
Cheezits	Macaroni and Cheese
Peanut Butter Granola	Sourdough Bread
Tabouli and Couscous	Popcorn w/ chocolate Quik powder
Pita Bread	Anything Layla makes
Indian Food	Chocolate Crossiants
Fried Bologna Sandwiches	Pepsi Vs. Coke
Noodles	Chinese tea
Three Bean Salad	Milkshakes
Cheetos and Fritos	Pep-O-Mints
Peppermint Patties	Chinese Foods
M&Ms	Cheese Pizza
Popsicles	Seasame Chicken
Orange Juice	Bagels
Macaroni and Cheese	Goggy's Famous Frozen Fruit Salad
Kit kats	Rice Dreams
Black bean Burritos	New England Clam Chowder
Nacho Cheese Popcorn	Richard Simmons snacks

Page thirty-three

And why just focus on your *fave* things? Here's Sara McCool's SOURPUSS list:

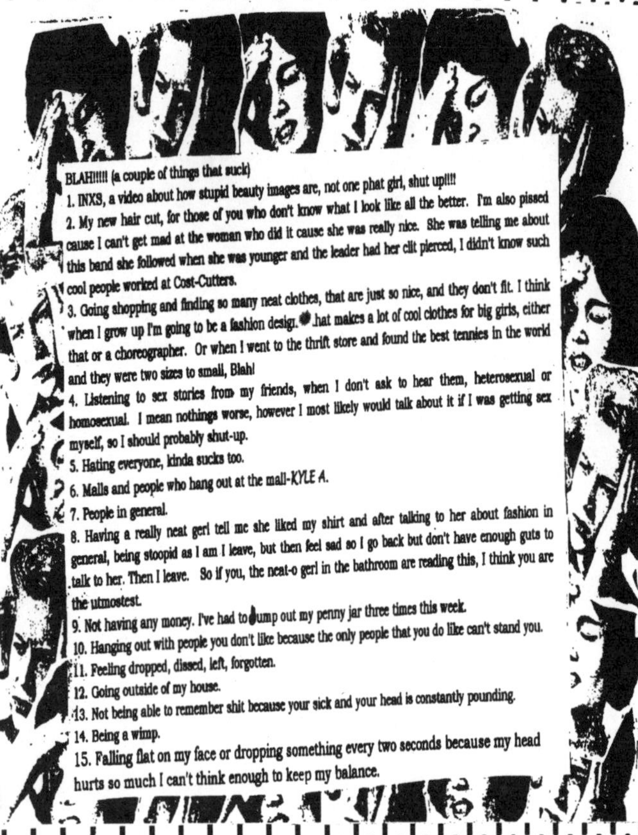

BLAH!!!!! (a couple of things that suck)
1. INXS, a video about how stupid beauty images are, not one phat girl, shut up!!!!
2. My new hair cut, for those of you who don't know what I look like all the better. I'm also pissed
cause I can't get mad at the woman who did it cause she was really nice. She was telling me about
this band she followed when she was younger and the leader had her clit pierced, I didn't know such
cool people worked at Cost-Cutters.
3. Going shopping and finding so many neat clothes, that are just so nice, and they don't fit. I think
when I grow up I'm going to be a fashion desig. hat makes a lot of cool clothes for big girls, either
that or a choreographer. Or when I went to the thrift store and found the best tennies in the world
and they were two sizes to small, Blah!
4. Listening to sex stories from my friends, when I don't ask to hear them, heterosexual or
homosexual. I mean nothings worse, however I most likely would talk about it if I was getting sex
myself, so I should probably shut-up.
5. Hating everyone, kinda sucks too.
6. Malls and people who hang out at the mall-*KYLE A.*
7. People in general.
8. Having a really neat gerl tell me she liked my shirt and after talking to her about fashion in
general, being stoopid as I am I leave, but then feel sad so I go back but don't have enough guts to
talk to her. Then I leave. So if you, the neat-o gerl in the bathroom are reading this, I think you are
the utmostest.
9. Not having any money. I've had to dump out my penny jar three times this week.
10. Hanging out with people you don't like because the only people that you do like can't stand you.
11. Feeling dropped, dissed, left, forgotten.
12. Going outside of my house.
13. Not being able to remember shit because your sick and your head is constantly pounding.
14. Being a wimp.
15. Falling flat on my face or dropping something every two seconds because my head
hurts so much I can't think enough to keep my balance.

ZINESTERS FAVES/OBSESSIONS/ HOBBIES/INSPIRATIONS

Thomas Christian, CHRONICLES OF DISORDER: "oboes, violins, rhythm of thought."

Mariah McDougall, age 17, MAGDALENE and REWM: "hands paper trash keys locks buttons pianos sounds voices blankets dads post it notes thumb tacks whole milk long drives bus rides early morning homegrown insomnia . . . doing it from scratch . . . familiar sidewalk cracks . . . knitting gum mail crassness."

Christian Merry, BLACK VIRGIN MARY COLORING BOOK: "I like drinking grape juice, and I like it so much I guess you could call it a hobby."

Abraham Katzman, FLAMING JEWBOY, I'M OVER BEING DEAD: "Platform shoes, Aquanet, June Jordan . . . low art, lipstick on walls and tinfoil showgirl outfits all inspire me, to what I don't know, but they inspire me."

Rebecca Schneider, (age "16 going on 120") TWO: ". . . tattoos, piercings, the unique, my mom, human nature . . . the usual."

Kim Cooper, age 29, SCRAM: ". . . neglected genius."

Otto von Stroheim, age 32, TIKI NEWS: "There is always a new Tiki to discover."

Tai, CICADA: ". . . the moon, nag champa incense . . . finding super-fun, nice, fuzzy people, especially other happy vegans, lovely unknown goth people . . . silver things and dark velvet . . . forests . . . chidren's books . . . chocolate tofutti . . . practicing subtle scathing sarcasm on annoying customers at work . . ."

Dan Moynihan, age 23, MICROBLAST: "I'm interested in the youthful spirit of obliviousness and exuberance, keeping open, changing and with eyes wide."

Lisa, age 18, BITCH DYKE WHORE: "My hobbies are my zine, riot grrrl, writing, changing the world, kicking ass, smashing patriarchy, ending homophobia, reading, and going to see bands."

Alissa Noonan, age 16, SPLIT ENDZ: ". . . screaming when i'm alone in my car."

Steve Lieber, age 29, THE STEVEN LIEBER SKETCHBOOK MINI: "The subject matter that presents itself to me. I'm partial to big, ancient objects and small, quirky people. Subtleties of light are important to me, as are nuances of character and snaky, linear rhythms."

Gretchen Christina Lowther, age 16, GOOD FAERIE: "Hope. Friends. Love. Burnt dreams. What I don't know yet and everything that could happen. Pleas for help. Soul. Chaos. Sound. Fear."

Michael, age 27, CULTURE FREAK: "I am inspired by the ever-present stupidity of human beings, the accelerated psycho-culture in which we are immersed at this point in history, and the increasing artificiality of life within that culture."

Biz Miller, age 19, THE GAME: "Sensationalist news stories inspire me to write about not being afraid. Things like the two girls at a punkrock show I went to who were dressed up like rosy-cheeked tatterdolls and swayed a druggy dance while the all-boy bands played inspire me to write about the difference between being a girl to be looked at and a girl to be heard."

RANTS

Rants are expressions of what pisses you off, written in a short, percussive style, or in long, wailing sentences. They can be silly or serious, personal or political, but they are always cathartic for the writer—and often the reader as well.

WHAT DO YOU WANT TO RANT ABOUT?

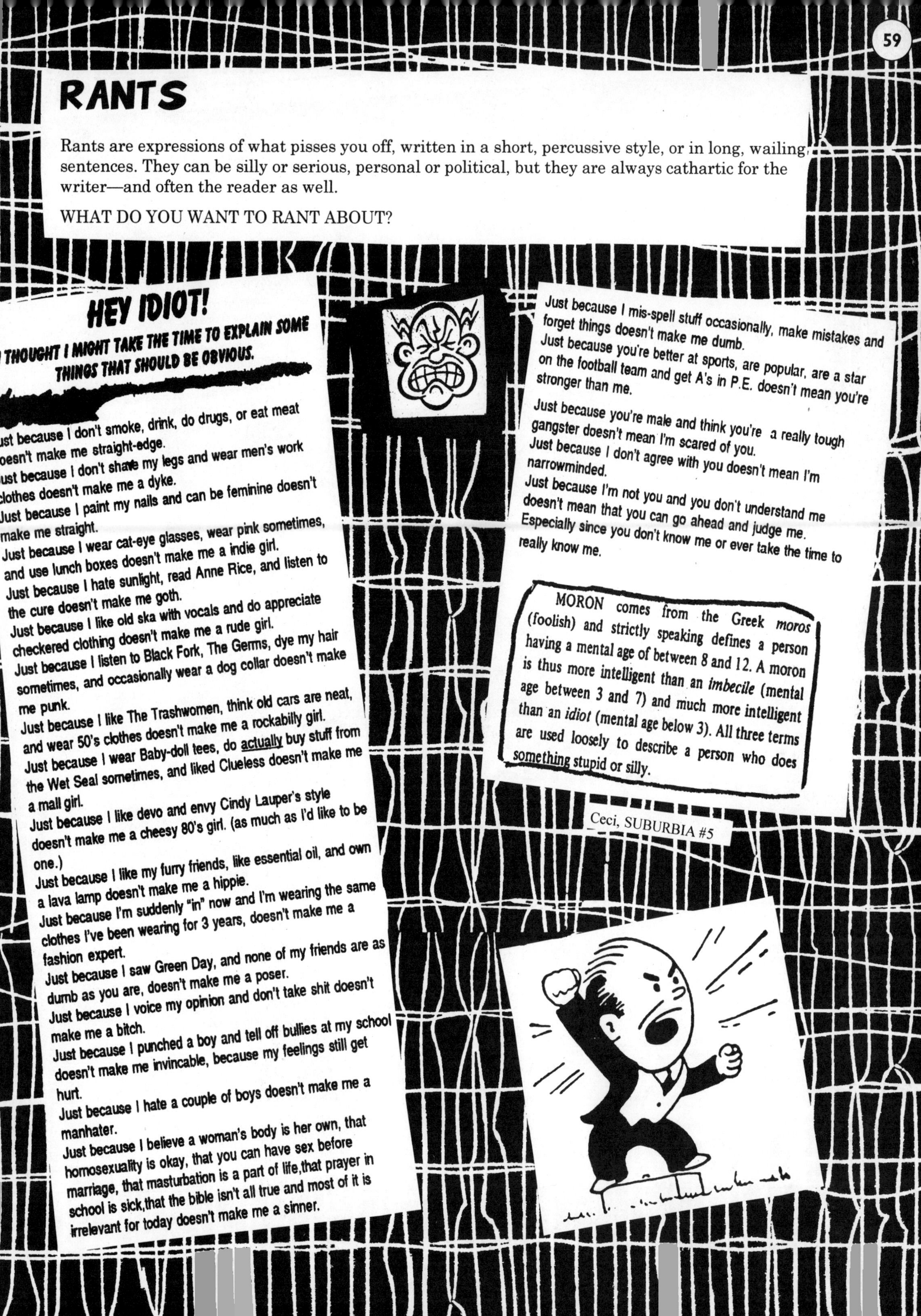

HEY IDIOT!

I THOUGHT I MIGHT TAKE THE TIME TO EXPLAIN SOME THINGS THAT SHOULD BE OBVIOUS.

Just because I don't smoke, drink, do drugs, or eat meat doesn't make me straight-edge.
Just because I don't shave my legs and wear men's work clothes doesn't make me a dyke.
Just because I paint my nails and can be feminine doesn't make me straight.
Just because I wear cat-eye glasses, wear pink sometimes, and use lunch boxes doesn't make me a indie girl.
Just because I hate sunlight, read Anne Rice, and listen to the cure doesn't make me goth.
Just because I like old ska with vocals and do appreciate checkered clothing doesn't make me a rude girl.
Just because I listen to Black Fork, The Germs, dye my hair sometimes, and occasionally wear a dog collar doesn't make me punk.
Just because I like The Trashwomen, think old cars are neat, and wear 50's clothes doesn't make me a rockabilly girl.
Just because I wear Baby-doll tees, do actually buy stuff from the Wet Seal sometimes, and liked Clueless doesn't make me a mall girl.
Just because I like devo and envy Cindy Lauper's style doesn't make me a cheesy 80's girl. (as much as I'd like to be one.)
Just because I like my furry friends, like essential oil, and own a lava lamp doesn't make me a hippie.
Just because I'm suddenly "in" now and I'm wearing the same clothes I've been wearing for 3 years, doesn't make me a fashion expert.
Just because I saw Green Day, and none of my friends are as dumb as you are, doesn't make me a poser.
Just because I voice my opinion and don't take shit doesn't make me a bitch.
Just because I punched a boy and tell off bullies at my school doesn't make me invincable, because my feelings still get hurt.
Just because I hate a couple of boys doesn't make me a manhater.
Just because I believe a woman's body is her own, that homosexuality is okay, that you can have sex before marriage, that masturbation is a part of life,that prayer in school is sick,that the bible isn't all true and most of it is irrelevant for today doesn't make me a sinner.

Just because I mis-spell stuff occasionally, make mistakes and forget things doesn't make me dumb.
Just because you're better at sports, are popular, are a star on the football team and get A's in P.E. doesn't mean you're stronger than me.

Just because you're male and think you're a really tough gangster doesn't mean I'm scared of you.
Just because I don't agree with you doesn't mean I'm narrowminded.
Just because I'm not you and you don't understand me doesn't mean that you can go ahead and judge me.
Especially since you don't know me or ever take the time to really know me.

MORON comes from the Greek *moros* (foolish) and strictly speaking defines a person having a mental age of between 8 and 12. A moron is thus more intelligent than an *imbecile* (mental age between 3 and 7) and much more intelligent than an *idiot* (mental age below 3). All three terms are used loosely to describe a person who does something stupid or silly.

Ceci, SUBURBIA #5

BY TONY FRENZEL

It's Hard to be Punk, When Your Mom Says No

One of the most annoying things in the world is when someone tries so hard to "fit in", or "connect" with someone or something, and then fail miserably at it. It's even more horrifying when it's your mom who is trying to "connect" with your own adventures in life and the popular culture. I'm 21 years old, and this is the bane of my existence—this is my curse.

My interest in today's punk/indie-rock music scene seems to be the source of my mother's attempt to "fit in" or "relate" with me. One night I decided to attend a Reverend Horton Heat/Melvins/White Zombie show in Chicago. When I told my mom (because parents always ask: "Where you are going?"), she responded with, "What do they do there? Isn't it called MUSHING?"

MUSHING???????? No mom, not quite. She went on to tell me about an article in the newspaper about a teenage boy who had died while moshing at some concert. Of course, the neurons in my mind were still erupting at the term "mushing". Now, I know my mom was just trying to be nice, but her ignorance on the subject—especially on the proper pronunciation of the term "moshing"—bit at me like a dog gnaws on a bone. I let is slide however, because, after all, she is sweet old mom.

About a week later, I picked my mom up from work. The car stereo was playing some Superchunk song. The following conversation took place:

MOM: "Is that you playing a song?"
ME: "Yeah, mom, that's me. How in the hell would I get on the radio?"
MOM: "Well, the voice sounds like you."
ME: "Well, it's not."
MOM: "Who's singing?"

Now I'm starting to get aggravated. Like she really cares who's singing or who the band is. Another pathetic attempt to "relate" to me.

ME: "It's Mac McCaughan from Superchunk."
MOM: "Superchip?"

Let's go mushing now, everybody's learning how ...

ME: "No, mom—'SuperCHUNK'."
MOM: "Superchunk? Chunk? As in the candy 'Chunky'?"

OK, now my blood is boiling.

ME: "Yes, mom, Superchunk."
MOM: "Oh. Why does he sing like that? His voice is off tune."
ME: "I don't know, mom; it's just the way he sings!"
MOM: "Is it suppose to sound like that?"
ME: "MOOOOOOOOOOOOOOOOM! STOP IT!"

What can a boy do to escape this persecution? Not much. About two minutes later my mom starts to dig her claws into me once again.

I had just gotten a haircut that day. The back, sides and the back of the top had been cut really short. Yet, my bangs still remained and draped both sides of my face. After many compliments from my friends and other misc. people on my haircut, my mom chips in with, "Why did you get that haircut, you look like a Hasidic Jew!" Thanks, mom. First of all, do you see friggin' braids down the sides of my face? Jesus christ (no pun intended), I did NOT look like a Hasidic Jew.

Of course, there have been many other attempts by my mom to relate to me and my interests, so I leave you with one more example of the patronizing treatment I receive from my mom. When I first started to publish my 'zine [*BLAH 'ZINE*], my mom countered with a barrage of my favorite questions—"What's a 'zine?" "What's it called? 'BLAH SEEN?' Is that like a magazine?" Shut up, mom, I love you and all ... but ...

Why this bothers me is a mystery. Perhaps I am short on patience. Perhaps I just don't want my mom to be involved in things in my life which I know she doesn't even give a damn about. Now, I love my mother, but her attempts to "connect" with my interests on the pop-culture level are futile, annoying and above all, patronizing. The worst part of it is, is that my mom—while trying to be nice—is totally and completely oblivious about her patronizing manner! I know I am not alone, and I assume that this type of thing has happened throughout time, to almost every child. So, let all the patronized children join hands and sing, "MOM!!!! JUST LEAVE ME ALONE!"

[Tony is also known as Mr. Moo of BLAH 'ZINE]

This is where we let our readers and contributors speak out on any subject—so if you have something to rant (or rave!) about, send it on up!!

From Cathy Rundell's FIZZ, #7

And I'd be a liar if I said class did not matter. And I'd be a liar if I said I didn't dislike you at times for all you have. No I'm not going to BS and say it's OK to make both of us comfortable. I've seen too many people work their lives away struggling for a hand hold and a little pride. And I've seen you cut them down and laugh at their clothes & their children's clothes. I've seen others pretend not to see them. Well I can see and I can feel and I've watched the homeless line up for soup in a town that supposedly has no homeless problem & I am not going to deny any longer aspects that aren't pleasant or aren't comfortable. Because they still exist - and they are still valid.

I've seen men die from years of mowing yr lawns and highway dividers. I've seen the shame in a neighbours eyes at a store because she can't find the right english word & you are treating her like that makes her stupid. I've seen the way you treat people differently and it makes me upset. And the differences you see are of race and of class - and I'm not pretending them away anymore. You can talk to me like a human being - you complain about the poor <who are according to you only poor because they want to be so - but no one wants to be poor> and that welfare trash. And I am them also but you say I'm different & better - and I know why you say this. The pale tint of my skin makes me better, makes it easier for you to understand how I might be unlucky & poor as opposed to lazy & poor.

Melissa Albach, LOOKING GLASS GIRL ZINE #3

Sometimes not even a piece of paper that says you can legally be in the U.S. helps you prove it. There is always a deep suspicion of Mexicans and other non-anglo cultures when it comes to legal status. Now more than ever this is the case because of Prop. 187 and other similar anti-immigrant legislation.

How can I be happy for my mom when this piece of paper will not make her look any less suspicious in anyone's eyes?

•SISI•

end.

Esta foto me la tomaron cuando iba al trabajo, pues iba enojada porque todos se me quedaban viendo.

-María de Jesus Nuñez

(OR IF YOU PREFER)

THIS PHOTOGRAPH WAS TAKEN WHILE I WAS ON MY WAY TO WORK, WELL I WAS REALLY ANGRY BECAUSE EVERY ONE WAS STARING AT ME.

-María de Jesus Nuñez

MARTA, MY MOM 30 yrs ago in Culiacan, Sinaloa

Sisi Medina and Maria Medina, ERACISM #1

RECIPES

Always wondered how to make a Polka Dot Choco-Mocha Eggless Raspberry-filled Peanut Butter Chip cake? (We have, so if anyone has the recipe, *please* send it to us!)

Why have recipes become a popular staple in zines? One reason may be due to the fact that so many more people these days are eating differently. A lot of zine recipes are for Vegan dishes (which contain no animal products at all).

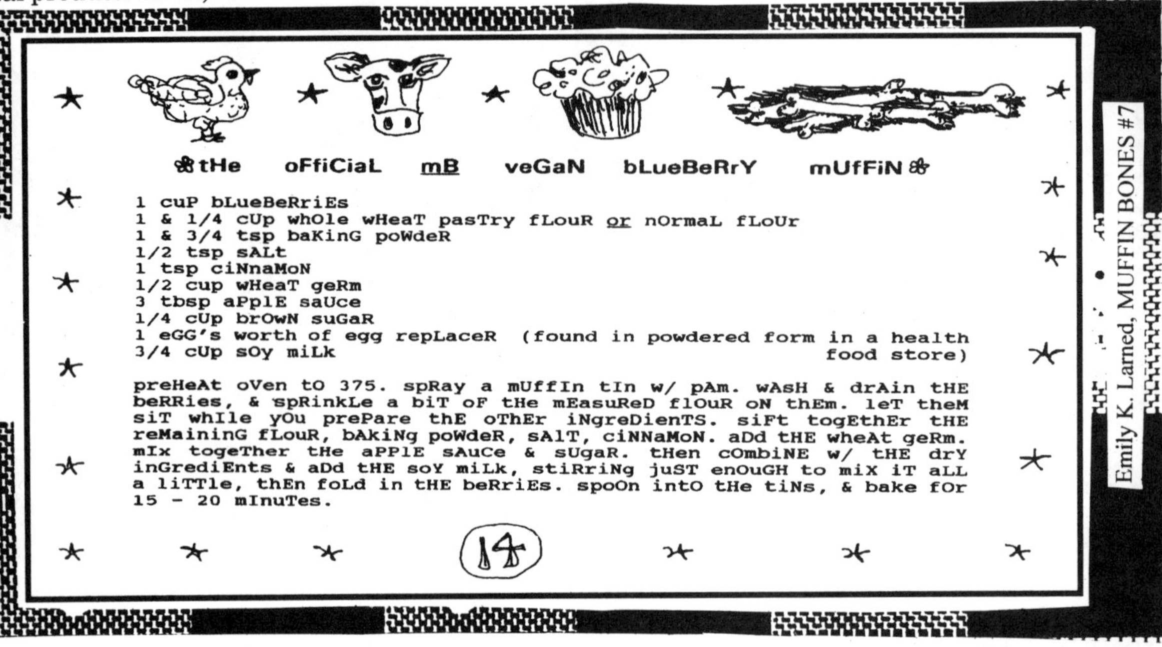

tHe oFfiCiaL mB veGaN bLueBeRrY mUfFiN

1 cuP bLueBeRriEs
1 & 1/4 cUp whOle wHeaT pasTry fLouR or nOrmaL fLoUr
1 & 3/4 tsp baKinG poWdeR
1/2 tsp sALt
1 tsp ciNnaMoN
1/2 cup wHeaT geRm
3 tbsp aPplE saUce
1/4 cUp brOwN suGaR
1 eGG's worth of egg repLaceR (found in powdered form in a health food store)
3/4 cUp sOy miLk

preHeAt oVen tO 375. spRay a mUffIn tIn w/ pAm. wAsH & drAin tHE beRRies, & spRinkLe a biT oF tHe mEasuReD flOuR oN thEm. leT theM siT whIle yOu prePare thE oThEr iNgreDienTS. siFt togEthEr tHE reMaininG fLouR, bAkiNg poWdeR, sAlT, ciNNaMoN. aDd tHE wheAt geRm. mIx togeTher tHe aPPlE sAuCe & sUgaR. tHen cOmbiNE w/ tHE drY inGrediEnts & aDd tHE soY miLk, stiRriNg juST enOuGH to miX iT aLL a liTTle, thEn foLd in tHE beRriEs. spoOn intO tHe tiNs, & bake fOr 15 - 20 mInuTes.

14

Emily K. Larned, MUFFIN BONES #7

Other zinesters just want to share the recipes that most stimulate their taste buds and fuel their bods while they are in the throes of zine mania.

ten easy recipies that are good for you

You'll never know until you try them. Dig in!

CHINESE BURRITOS

*ready-to-eat flour tortillas
*La Choy fancy mixed vegtables
*Miracle Whip

After draining off the water, place chinese vegtables in a microwave-safe dish and warm for two minutes. Spread Miracle Whip on the tortilla. Add vegtables and wrap up carefully.

CHEESEY CHEEKS

*grated mozzarella
*mayonnaise
*sliced english muffins

Mix cheese with mayonnaise and spread on muffin halves. Broil until cheese is bubbly.

SOOPER BREAKFAST SHAKE

*4 cm chunk of tofu
*1/4 cup of milk
*1/3 cup of crushed pineapple or fruit of your choice
*two spoonfuls of whip cream

Blend together. This shake tastes totally rad and keeps you energized through the day.

TOOTH COATING

*2 cups brown sugar
*1 stick of butter
*2 eggs
*1 1/2 cups of flour
*1 tsp. vanilla

Mix sugar and butter until creamy. Add beaten eggs, flour and vanilla. Cook at 325 F for 35-40 minutes. Cool and cut into jolly animal shapes.

FRENCH HOT DOGS

*hot dog bun
*string cheese
*dijon mustard

Spread dijon mustard onto the inside of the bun. Add string cheese. Microwave for 40 seconds or until cheese is melted. Transfer to a shallow pan with butter and fry both sides of the bu[n]

CHEESE AND CARROT JOLLY

*Lawash whole wheat flat bread
*prepared baby carrots
*assorted cheese

Fill center of flat bread with the cheese of your choice. I reccomend a mild white cheese, like jarlesburg. Add whole baby carrots and roll up. Microwave for one minute or until cheese melts.

MAKE MY OWN DAMN PEPPERMINTS

1/2 cups of sugar
/2 cup of water
egg whites
/4 tsp. cream of tartar
nint extract

oil water and sugar until it threads. eat egg whites stiffly. Pour water and ugar concoction onto mixture of egg vhites and cream of tartar. Add 10 rops mint extract and beat until really tiff. Drop onto buttered wax paper.

PANAMANIAN DRUG SCHOONER

*Granny apples
*peanut butter
*1/2 cup Rice Krispies
*cheddar cheese

Cut apples in half and remove cores, leaving a cavity. Mix peanut butter and Rice Krispies and fill the cavity in the apple. Fashion tiny dope crates with the cheddar and place on top.

PARTY NIPPLES

*one banana
*smooth peanut butter
*chocolate chips

Cut the banana into centimeter thick rounds. Dab peanut butter onto banana circles and top with a chocolate chip. *For an extra hip 90's version, pierce nipple with a toothpick and serve

Molly Aviva Brodak, THE BEST OF THE FLABBY ARMS

- Raid your mom or dad's, boyfriend or girlfriend's recipe file. Ask the cook at the health food deli for their tofu-noodle-strudel recipe. MAKE UP YOUR OWN!

FASHION

Are you tired of having the mainstream media dictate to you what to wear to look foxy? *You* know what you think is foxy. So why not revolutionize fashion with a concoction of your own and publicize it shamelessly and with aplomb in your zine?

Do you love Converse? Celebrate their springy magic slammingness in your zine like Josie does in A GREAT DAY FOR UP. She makes her fashion rave a true ode to all-star feet.

If thrift fashions are your specialty like they are Al Hoff's in THRIFT SCORE or Stephan Drennan's in STEPHAN'S LITTLE BOOK OF CHARITY SHOPPING, guide your reader through the stained and smelly rejects to find the treasures.

Or if anti-fashion is your passion, rant on!

FASHION
items i've grown an affinity for!
[next issue - my bag fetish! :)]
glamour* glasses*
bought @ a street fair on greenwich ave. for $5
black cat's eyes
snagged these in montreal
faux tortoise-shell
and for that matter women's pyjamas
i found this in the basement closet. i remember my mom used to wear this! it's a beautiful purple and very satiny. mmm...
men's pyjamas
these have cute parts, too.
silk Chinese purses
my grandmother gets me these
fat laces!
another montreal find. saw them in a cheap shoe store & snagged 8 pairs cheap!

Lauren Martin, YOU MIGHT AS WELL LIVE #3

12

EVER WONDER WHERE RING COLLECTOR'S GET THEIR RINGS? HERE'S A CHART I'VE MADE OF MY FAVORITE RINGS AND WHERE I GOT THEM.

RING	DESCRIPTION	ORIGIN
	Lime green center that really reminds me of Kiwi Italian soda. The petals are metal.	A weird little gift shop in Hillcrest. It was $12
	It's a mood ring with little sparkles inside. what else is there to say?	A Ramona Street Fair about 4 years ago. It was $2
	It's silver and flowery and it's heavey.	It says it's from Korea, but my dad found it in a parking lot.
	Really cheap and old and plastic. I'm surprised it's still intact.	who Knows?
	Iz plazteec. And purple. with little fake diamonds around it	My boyfriend got it for me at a 25¢ machine at Payless

Serra Sewitch, MOON FUZZ #4

MAKE YR OWN STUFF

Rebecca D. Dillion, age 21, is one zine diva of DIY arts and crafts promotion. Why not be like her, and her VELVET GRASS contributors, and teach your readers how to make things like panty purses, paper girl dolls, sparkly hair gear, trading card surprises, cardboard heads, and your own shrinky dinks?

let's have some
fun
with
DUCT TAPE
Marissa
of NOTHING, inc.
teaches you how to
make your own
duct tape
mary janes
YOU WILL NEED:
a roll of silver duct tape
a pair of inexpensive, black cotton "Chinese shoes"
cutting tools:
• sharp scissors
• Swiss Army Knife
WHAT'CHA DO:
cut several strips of tape, about 3 inches long, ½ in. to 1 in. wide. Use thicker strips when wrapping large areas of the shoe, and thin strips for reinforcement and for wrapping the strap.
start taping at the back of the shoe, work along one of the sides to the toe of the shoe, and up around the other side.
wrap the strap last, being careful not to make the tip too thick.
have fun wearing your cool new shoes!
DUCT TAPE
dream
I love duct tape so! The other night I dreamt that my sister and I received identical packages in the mail from our grandparents that were completely wrapped in DUCT TAPE!

Marissa Falco and Rebecca Dillon, VELVET GRASS #21

CONTESTS AND POLLS

Involve your readers by having them use their heads for a contest, or find out what's rattling around in there with a poll.

In GIRL DETECTIVE #1, Robyn E. Lee sponsors a sleuthy contest...

Know the code!!!

Secret codes have been used for centuries, harboring messages that can be tough to crack. But none are impossible. Below is the key to a famous code, the Pig pen Cipher. This code has been used by several secret societites. Most famous-the Freemasons! Yes, those crazy kooks that have infiltrated every aspect of our society. They teach you at school and run the government. They even killed the first president of the USA! And who knows? Maybe the secret plans for that assassination were written in their ouwn secret code. So learn it, and beat them at their own game.

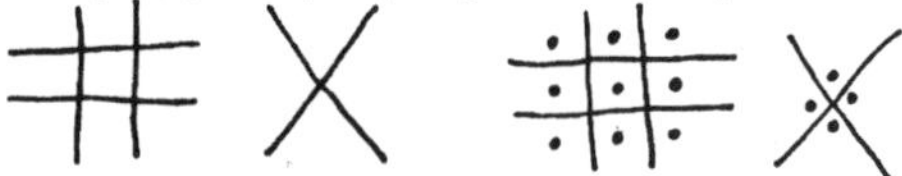
= Know The Code!

Sure, it looks confusing, but it is actually simple. First, draw a tic-tac-toe grid, followed by a large X. Repeat, placing a dot in each compartment:

Next, place a letter of the alphabet in each of the 26 compartments:

Now, you have the key. The letters are represented by the lines and dots that surround them. Here is your new alphabet:

A B C D E F G H I J K L M N O P Q R S T U V W X Y Z

If, during one of your mysteries, you come across a secret message using this code, simply draw the key to decipher it. Or, use it to make your own messages. Someday, when your a great sleuth like me or Nancy Drew, you may be able to memorize it.

"My name is Robyn E. Lee, and that may or may not be my real name. Due to my sensitive occupation, I would rather leave that under wraps."

GIRL DETECTIVE Robyn, started her zine to pay homage to the famous and revered girl detective, Nancy Drew.

CONTEST

The first person to return the following code correctly deciphered will win their own Girl Detective T-shirt!!!

In each issue of STOP, a zine that was published in the mid-'80s, the editors included readers' choices for the 40 funniest/coolest things.

Why not do a poll and see what your readers' fave things are? What are they listening to? What are they reading? Ask them yourself.

THIS IS IT! THE END OF AN ERA! THE VERY LAST READERS' CHOICES FOR THE FUNNIEST/COOLEST THINGS!

1. CASH MONEY — CABBAGE!
2. ROLLER DERBY — HELL ON WHEELS

3. Low Riders — MI JEFITO ES BAJITO!

4. ROCKY & BULLWINKLE — A SQUIRREL & A MOOSE
5. the 3 STOOGES — NYUK NYUK!

6. HOWARD STERN! — NY'S MAD DOG D.J. 3-7PM 66AM

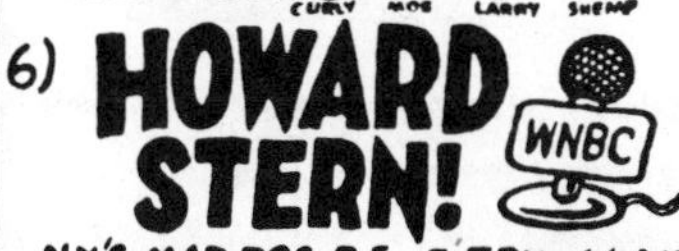

7. ANGRY SAMOANS — PISSED-OFF POLYNESIANS
8. TEX AVERY — KING OF CARTOONS!

9. THE CRAMPS — A PSYCHOBILLY BAND

10. Felix THE CAT — A WONDERFUL, WONDERFUL CAT

11. SAD SACK — A HARVEY COMIC BY FRED RHOADS
12. ETCH-A-SKETCH — HOW THE STOP! ARTISTS LEARNED TO DRAW

13. JOHNNY QUEST — HANNA-BARBERA'S APEX OF ANIMATION
14. ¡TACO! BUBBLE GUM — A REAL FLAVOR FROM AMUROLCO OF IL.

15. LLOYD LINDSAY YOUNG — INDEPENDENT NETWORK NEWS — A CULT WEATHERMAN
16. HOBOKEN cinema — BLOOD GUTS SLEAZE — GOREMONGER'S MOVIE HOUSE
17. THE CAVITY CREEPS — KIRBY ANIMATED T.V. COMMERCIAL
18. ED KOCH — NY'S MAD DOG MAYOR
19. The LYRES — A CULT BAND
20. TOR — AN ACTOR'S ACTOR

21. WEIRDO MAGAZINE — A COMIC BY, FOR & ABOUT WEIRDOS
22. SPINAL TAP — A BAND, A MOVIE, AN OPERATION

23. CHESTERFIELD KINGS — A BITCHEN-ASS GARAGE BAND

24. The PRODUCERS — A MEL BROOKS PRODUCTION
25. ANDY KAUFMAN — CONCEPTUAL COMEDIAN R.I.P.
26. LUMPY RUTHERFORD — BEAVER'S OBESE BUDDY
27. the Dating Game — PUBLIC SERVICE TELEVISION
28. HERMAN'S HERMITS — THE NOW SOUND
29. John Candy — LAFF RIOT COMEDIAN
30. PSYCHOTRONIC ENCYCLOPEDIA OF FILM — AN INDISPENSABLE REFERENCE BOOK
31. METS — NY'S MAD DOG BALL TEAM
32. MASHED POTATOES — FUN FOOD
33. THE Ben Vaughn COMBO — INDESCRIBABLE
34. VIC & SADE — OLD RADIO COMEDY SHOW
35. SQUA TRONT — GREAT EC FANZINE
36. THE FABULOUS MOOLA — RECENTLY DETHRONED WRESTLING QUEEN
37. Top Secret — LAFF RIOT SPY SPOOF
38. THE RAUNCH HANDS — AN AMERICAN BAND
39. Fritzi Ritz — HUBBA HUBBA! NANCY'S FOXY AUNT
40. Brother Theodore — A PHILOSOPHER

A SPECIAL NOTE TO THOSE WHO DIDN'T VOTE: YOU APATHETIC BUMS! YOU REALLY BLEW IT!! YOU'LL NEVER GET ANOTHER CHANCE LIKE THIS AS LONG AS YOU LIVE!! SERVES YOU RIGHT!

REVIEWS

Zines can include reviews of movies, books, music and/or concerts.

the innocence mission...

february 13, 1996. borders books and music.

february 13, 1996. caravan of dreams.

oh, dear goodness. words do not exist to describe my love for the innocence mission. they are such a lovely, lovely, lovely band! and i nearly passed out with joy at the opportunity to see them play in such an intimate setting as a bookstore (tsunami played there a year ago, which was equally thrilling). the first thing i noticed was how really cute the guys were. no offense to them or anything, but in a lot of the pictures i have of them, they look old. (poor lighting?) but then karen arrived, and you could have knocked me over with a feather. she is the sort-of girl that i would have secretly admired in high school but would have never had the courage to talk to. she is absolutely beautiful in such a calm, serene way that just being in her presence made me feel awkward and immature in comparison. photos do not do her justice! they opened with "surreal" one of my ultimate favourites and then proceeded to play material off their latest album, glow. the set was much too short in my opinion, but they were in a rush to get to their next show...

the innocence mission at borders books and music in fort worth

I love this picture because everyone looks so cute, but I accidentally missed Don in this shot which damn near breaks my heart. They were so nice as they signed CD's and posters. Two people in a row asked Kerin if she knew who the girls were on the cover of Glow, and it didn't even annoy her! And I told them about my house, and they were so sweet and excited for me, like they actually cared or something!

after the show, i scurried out to the parking lot and hurried over to caravan of dreams, a most beautiful club in downtown fort worth. it reminds me of a movie set, with the dramatic stage curtains and dusky atmosphere. i wish i could have taken pictures, but i didn't want to risk having my film confiscated. in any case, they made up for their short set at borders with a wide, comprehensive performance of their past releases. i became giggly during the first chords of "curious" and karen made me all tearful when she played "birds of wonder". the entire show made me feel so wonderful and light, the same feeling i get when i watch an audrey hepburn movie. and then what should they play next but a cover of "moon river" from audrey's film breakfast at tiffany's? i swear, it was so emotional for me i almost burst into tears. this was one of the best concerts i have been to for a while.

Janice Headly, COPACETIC #1

In MUFFIN BONES #15, Emily K. Larned reviews her world!

reviews

"honeychain" & "two step" (songs) tracks 10 & 12 respectively on throwing muses' the real ramona and quite simply hauntingly beautiful: the sparity of tanya's guitar melody and then the crashing drum that crushes my chest right in. turn off the lights and open the windows and with the influx of cold clear winter air, all hearts, everywhere, are broken.

nail buffer (cosmetic tool) grey to scruff out ridges. white to smooth off scruff. pink to gloss until your nails are a vampiric sort of shiny, a blushed sort of sheen like white zinfandel in a wine glass. like transparent nail polish but better because it is simply your own nail, amplified.

of human bondage (film) so old that the print is brown and white, not black and white, and bette davis is small and beautiful instead of horrid and terrifying and decrepit, like in whatever happened to baby jane?. and the near-tragic story, so carefully told: finally, not a film about women only loving men who are bad to them, and not the simple inverse either: instead, a story about passionate love and how we do not always or often love the ones who love us best, no matter what our gender.

strawberry chapstick (winter necessity) the first lip gloss, that taste of playground kiss, recess, puffy primary colored parkas, and thick nylon moon boots.

the secret stars the secret stars (album) perfectly gorgeous spare lyricism: very nearly almost just guitars and geof and jodi, intelligent cryptic lyrics that tell story after story. and when the two of them perform live, the room is dark except for the light from their old elegant standing lamp.

spinach (vegetable) cooked of course: that thick green texture and rich color, boiled with onion, cumin, and turmeric: the most underrated of vegetables. popeye was more right than he knew.

the shop around the corner (film) so charming and sweetly funny, in the way that only a very young jimmy stewart can be: budapest at christmas time, and through an intellectual correspondence two lovely young people, despite themselves,

EMILY K. LARNED'S

MUFFIN BONES was listed by *F5* as one of the ten most popular zines in the country. Reading this 20-year-old's vibrant prose is like tasting the coffee with a shot of vanilla that she sips and hearing the PJ Harvey album she's listening to. Queen of Muffin Bones also draws in a quirky, dynamic style. The benefits of doing MUFFIN BONES? ". . . the confidence to believe that I can make a living (and more importantly, a life) in the arts, completely independent of mainstream culture. Zines, and what they represent, are everything to me. I cannot emphasize this enough."

Writing reviews of other zines can be helpful to your readers, fellow zinesters, and also to *you*. Someone will probably be more likely to mention you if you mention them! It's good to include a few of the details that make the zine you are reviewing unique and worth the read. Remember: all zines are works of art and expression, and deserve acknowledgment. Their purpose in life is not to be judged. If you can't think of something positive to say, you don't *have* to review it. You can simply mention it, list the contents, ignore it altogether, or consider the "sophisticated dis." You can be critical, but remember, also try to have some tact and compassion when you express why you don't like it.

SOME ZINE SCENE REVIEWS . . .

- RAGDOLL: Cheryl Tapper writes about "Queens of '70s psychedelic children's TV," self defense, Riot Grrrl, sizeism, Diamanda Galas, and Sky Dancers—all with depth and grace.

- BILLY'S MITTEN: A cute teenybopper zeeny by one cute teenybopper Teresa Mitten (aka Teresa Miteen, Miss Mitten/Miteen or Miss Ghosty for her band the GHOSTY GRAMS.) It features "trading cards" of kids at school whom she has crushes on, as well as fun accounts of her romps with best friend Seth Bee. Together, they are champions of the "teen revolution."

- SELL OUT BOY: Jose Torres writes exposing pieces, then cuts and pastes them to make a per-boy zine that cuts right to the heart and sticks there.

- TWO: by Rebecca (Bex) Schneider and Casey Butterfield. Honest revelations and potent poetry by and about two slinkstresses. Homages to girls who rock (Ani DeFranco), write (Pleasant Gehman), and are unreal (Artemis).

- **MAD GIRL:** by Emily Anne. A striking layout using her own black and white woodcut-like drawings, and just-as-strong words about love, sex, and grrrls.

- **THE CHEESE STANDS ALONE:** Edmund Scientific uses elegant/kitschy collage clip-art to illustrate pieces about jello, finding a "homeless deity," having blue hair, and "the 20 absolute worst ways to die." Plus, he included a fabric sample, crazy kitty stickers, and a library book card with the issue he sent.

- **HERO GRRRL:** Jessica Wilbur's rad newsletter-style zine gives grrrls plenty to think about and plenty to do. Play along with guitar charts for Jewel songs or check out the hot web sites Jessica recommends.

- **CEILINGS PEEL:** "GIRLS RULE" and so does Heather Anne Burnett. She writes about grrrl conventions and her commitment to Riot Grrrl, struggles with her anti-zine mom, and dishes a flirty U.P.S. man.

COMIX

You can always give your zine sheen with some hand-drawn images.

Excerpt from piece in issue #1

Twenty five-year-old James Masente chose to create UNREQUITED LOVE THEATER as a way to deal with frustrating romantic encounters and "to purge myself of the psychological demons that haunt me." But after the first issue, he "kept seeing girls who were identical to the one in the story—scary." Now he's obsessed with "swing dancing and finding a girl who will appreciate me for my neurosis."

Excerpt from piece by Emily Anne, ANGST GIRL #2

inside storu **Confidential** HUSH-HUSH

PERSONAL WRITING

Besides per-zines, there are zines that may just include a per-piece or two. Per-stuff is often either wildly euphoric or what Mariah McDougall calls "bloody raw sorrow" and "celestial tragedy."

Maybe the single most important aspect of the zine revolution is this revelation of what hurts. By sharing our dark secrets, we may be able to heal someone else's.

4-30-96 i hate it when people refer to me as a rape victim.in webster's dictionary the first definition of victim is a "beast for sacrifice". i think the term makes me sound pathetic and helpless. i prefer to think of myself as a survivor.

She cultivates homemaking skills.

Lisa Oppedyk, BITCH DYKE WHORE #1

TRUE Life Secrets

TRUTH DARE EXPOSED

CONFESSIONS PRIVATE STORY SHOCKING NEWS

PRIVATE LIVES *UNCENSORED*

TRUTH DARE EXPOSED TRUE Life Secrets inside storu Confidential HUSH-HUSH CONFESSIONS PRIVATE STORY SHOCKING NEWS UNCENSORED PRIVATE LIVES THE Lowdown THE FACTS THEY DARE NOT TELL YOU

My Secret by alissa

This is the first time I am writing or talking, for that matter, about a subject that was apart of 2 years of my life and always will be a part of my life. I just started to read stephanie's zine kill supermodels and it made me think. I don't know if I'll have the courage to print this or not but I'll try. This is about my case of Anorexia. That word is so hard for me to say and it makes me cringe as I write it. This article will probably upset my best friends because I have never admitted to or talked about having this disease with anyone except for my sister. I was scared to tell anyone. I was scared I'd get their sympathy. I was scared that if someone brought up my name someone else would say, oh...her...she's really fucked up she was anorexic. I was scared of accepting that I was sick. I've only accepted that recently. This is not my story of how I won my battle against the barbie stereotype it's how I fell for it. This is not a cry for help or sympathy. This is to help my sisters that I see getting hurt and hurting themselves every day. I'll start my story now. It began in sixth grade (5 years ago). I was fat. There's no other way to describe it. Not huge but fat.

People noticed. Boys, one in particular, would make fun of me constantly. Whenever I passed by- Thunder thighs! Thump! Thump! This one guy who I will call Greg never ever left me alone. I cried all of the time because of him. My aunt pulled me aside at a party to tell me I'd be pretty if I'd only loose some weight. One day when I was sitting in my room putting on a shirt, my father walked in and his eyes bulged and he said something along the lines of "oh my god." He told me he 'd quit smoking if I lost weight and I'd be pretty if I did because he saw a pretty me under the fat. He never quit smoking. This is not an attack on my dad because I know he loves me and just thought I'd be happier if I was thin. I actually thought I was pretty until everybody told me I was fat. I guess nobody knew that. It hurts me to write this because I know how guilty and hurt he feels that he hurt me. The only time I ever saw my father cry was when he found out how much he had hurt me in therapy. My mom would often say things that would make me cry, but then say she didn't mean anything by them which she probably didn't. I had such a low self-esteem by that point that I interpreted anything as you 're fat. My sister never said anything to me but just looking at how skinny and popular she was made me feel worthless. I hated myself and everyone else. I cried a lot. Then, I started my dieting. It started with faithfully giving up all junk food for lent and built up to 0 fat a day. I even ate smaller portions of healthy choice because 2 grams of fat was too much for me. I ran to my mom's room crying and holding a bunch of 'Teen magazines saying how beautiful the models were and how I would never be that thin. I scared her to death she told me to stop it because half of those models were anorexic and I would be too but that seemed too It-Could-Never-Happen-To-Me and I didn't believe her. I weighed about 110 pounds and was 5 feet tall in 6th grade. My goal was to weigh 70 pounds. I tried and tried for months and got a lot thinner. Everyone said I looked great so I kept going. I could look even better. I got really excited about my first day of seventh grade. I could show off my new body. People didn't even recognize me. One girl said I should stop or I would become anorexic. I laughed. I said I was just getting taller. When I was talking to a girl the same size I used to be Greg came up to her and said "Now it 's your turn to loose weight." I felt great and bad at the same time because I was the new me and saw the old me at the same time. I looked sick. My parents got scared and took me to the doctor for a physical for gym. My mom sat there anxiously waiting for my doctor to weigh me. She (my doctor) looked shocked and told my mom that I weighed 85 pounds and was 5'2 or 3 I forgot. She told my mom to take me across the street to get my blood tested and my heart monitored to see if I hadn't hurt my heart. It was O.K. She told my mom that she had 5 days to get me help or she'd report her to the state. Something we later found out she had no right to say. My mom was crying. I was mad, trying not to cry, and glaring at my doctor. I hated her at that moment. At that moment, I saw a young doctor anxious to get her hands on something serious who was exaggerating. After the appointment my mom took me to a pancake house. I took my first bite out of a very fattening apple pancake and said This is going to be fun I was very wrong. I went home and watched movies of me when I was fat crying because I didn't want to look like that again. My mom called her family and friends "for support" I thought she just wanted people to feel sorry for HER, her when I was the one suffering. It took me at least a year or two to trust her again and talk to her about my problems with her again. I didn't want to be talked about. I didn't think I had a problem and stayed in denial for years. Three days later therapy started. Family Therapy because they insisted it was a cry for help because of family problems when it wasn't at all. They never changed their minds. To me it was torture because it's hard to get help when you don't think you have a problem. My therapist told me what other anorexic girls are like and to her automatically that was me. I was stereotyped. It hurt to be one of those stories you read about an anorexic girl in 'Teen 2 pages before an ad for how to get the perfect body in 60 days. I hated my therapist and I told her everytime I saw her. Everytime I saw her I cried and cried. She made me feel like everything was my fault. She wouldn't hear anything about what others did to me and believe it. She was always against me, always sided with my family. I didn't gain weight because I was getting better, I gained weight because I didn't want to go to therapy anymore, because they'd hospitalize me if I didn't. My teachers cornered me in a room and said they were concerned. I knew that only one of them was, the rest just wanted some hot gossip. So I kept my mouth shut. I've spent five years with this secret because I can't trust anyone with it. I couldn't talk to my therapists because I hated them and couldn't trust them. I was gaining weight and going to the doctor for weigh-ins. One day she told me she got another anorexic girl like "do you know her?" One day in the hall I heard somebody say to Greg, "She lost a lot of weight." and he said "yea. but she's gaining it all back." it was like, "yes, but do you know when you thought I looked good I was anorexic and it was partly because of you?" It made me hate our society I could only look good if I was anorexic. I'm healthy again and I'm not fat. I'll never be totally happy with myself and never eat as much as others for fear of the pain I went through but I'm not fat. That's not my lesson to you but to show you what you don't want to become. To show you what I do to myself to make myself acceptable to the society that wants hourglass figures out of women. It's sick. I'm not unhappy anymore because it's my lifestyle and I guess I'll be OK as long as I don't get obsessive. I, just like anyone else, shouldn't have to settle for this but it's easier. Easier for me because I'm weak and can't put up with being tormented, but I'm not a good example all of you stand up and fight because we are all beautiful no matter what anyone says. Even me. I'm scared for my friends because a few are reminding me of myself and I don't want them to go through that. The girl who told me I was going to become anorexic is now anorexic herself. I just want to tell you grrrls that if this sounds like you, STOP! before it's too late you are beautiful and if you insist on losing weight, do it for yourself and not some boy and see a dietitian and do it safely. It's not worth the pain.

Alissa Noonan, SPLIT ENDZ #2

MISCELLANEOUS

Here are a few more things that can show up in zines.

- **EVENT LISTINGS**: Musician coming to town? Grrl Convention or gathering? Sk8 competition?
- **PROJECT LISTINGS**: Looking for writers to collaborate with? A bass player for your band? Why not use your zine to network?
- **SURPRISES**: barrettes, posters, stickers, patches, valentines, sequins. JELLY SLIDE included a record on thin red vinyl! In an issue of RANTEX, they kept two pages blank and glued different found objects onto each zine (poker chip, used greeting card, news clipping).
- **REPRINTS OF ARTICLES**: From '50s dating etiquette to '90s safe sex tips. (See page 92 for the facts on copyright).
- **SOUNDTRACKS**: A list of what the zinester was listening to while designing (or *dezine-ing!*) their issue.
- **TRULY MISC. STUFF**: Those one-of-a-kind-things that make zines all so unique:
  - √ In one issue of CROTCHET,Shelly includes a centerfold of her footprint in ink.
  - √ Tina Henry, of RESTAURANT FUEL, features a mail order flea market where she sells items she's collected.
  - √ Sabrina's algebra home-work makes an appearance in PEPSI DEGENERA TION.
  - √ In FLABBY ARMS, Molly Aviva Brodak interviews her second-grade sister.

OH MAGOO you've done it again!

I used to get so excited when the opening song for the Mickey Mouse Club Show would come on. My fervor would build as a sunburst would appear on the screen with a tiny Mickey head in the center. Mickey's face would get larger. I'd get even more thrilled. Then, right before his face was to disappear, I'd press my lips against the screen with a big "SMOOCH!" To Mickey, I was completely devoted and completely loyal.

Now, though, my tastes have become more sophisticated and diverse and my imaginary love-interests are more varied and complex. To adequately explain this, I'm going to use Robert Sternberg's Triangular Theory of Love, which posits that all relationships are mixtures of 3 elements: Passion, Imtimacy, and Commitment. Please note, though, that I'm sticking only to mainstream cartoon characters. To discuss my crushes on Underground cartoon characters would be far too complex and people might confuse my attraction to a character with an attraction to its creator and Heaven knows I don't need any more of those kinds of rumors floating about. Besides, this is all merely speculative. I don't actually know how a relationship with a cartoon character would actually work out.

CALVIN by Bill Watterson
Passion, Intimacy, and Commitment = Consummate Love
Lured in by his vivid imagination, I'd happily replace Hobbes as his quietly snide sidekick. Passion? We'd sled together, share hot chocolate and get way too excited about it. Intimacy? He'd tell me all his secrets and I'd never tell anyone. Commitment? With him by my side, how could I hope for anything better?

SCHROEDER by Charles Schulz
Passion and Commitment = Hollywood Love
I'd be his most ardent fan, but, alas, my tastes would run too far below his strict standards to be allowed into his emotional world. Nevertheless, I'd answer his every call and accommodate his every whim & as long as I'm the only woman in his life, everything will be fine.

TINTIN by Hergé
Intimacy and Commitment = Companionate Love
When I think of Tintin, I imagine him sitting in a chair in my apartment telling me about his adventures while Snowy and Zinc chase eachother around the room. Then, we'd get interrupted by a call from Captain Haddock. Tintin would hug me goodbye and promise to see me again when he returned.

LINUS by Charles Schulz
Passion and Intimacy = Romantic Love
Sure, I'd be swept away by his sincerity, but this little fellow lacks one thing, charisma. I'm certain that our discussions and emotions would be deep and intense, but I'd be so attracted to his friend, Schroeder, that I couldn't fully commit myself to him.

NANCY by Ernie Bushmiller
Intimacy = Friendly Love
I've been compared to her too many times to find her attractive and I don't think she really needs my commitment, since Sluggo and Aunt Fritzi are always there for her. It would be fun, however, to get together with her for sodas every now and then and talk about our problems.

MR. MAGOO (I don't know who created him)
Commitment only = Empty Love
Sure this guy's a real cutie, but the charm of his senility would wear thin after fretting over his near misses with death. He'd constantly misunderstand me. He's too frail for affection. And he'd continually upset me by mistaking me for others. I'd take care of him, though, when his nephew wasn't around.

SMITHERS by Matt Groening
Passion = Infatuation
Could there be a more attractive man in all of cartoondom? The glasses, the overbite, the bow-tie... and I'm in love. Unfortunately, his interests lie elsewhere, so my passion for him, no matter how intense, would be painfully one-sided.

Mary Burt, SAD #4

Lamp that's a plant that's a lamp:

Here's a swell story that came into TS HQ. It's a marvelous tale cause you can just feel the frantic excitement bouncing off the page as Paul W. of AZ careens from the thrift disappointments (not for sale, broken) to the small victories that drive us all to thrift – the sighting, the buying, the cleaning and fixing, the displaying. In the best of traditions of thrift shopping and exploration, Paul is happy at home with his functioning Plamp, but still remains charmed by its mysteries and the circumstances by which he came by it.

This boutiquey type thrift opened in town and as of late, they have a somewhat offensive but kinda OK installation dubbed "Retro Metro." Anyway, a year or so ago, there was a ghastly fab Plamp which stood near the racks marked very definitely **"NOT FOR SALE. STORE DISPLAY ONLY."** Phooey, I said. So I had a little talk with the manager and basically queried as to the fate/destiny of the Plamp after the eventual demise of the Retro-Metro nonsense. Manager was a little peeved that I was panning the whole Retro-Metro notion but polite and insistent that said-Plamp would **never** sell.

Months go by. I look at it. The manager tells me how so many folks have offered lotsa money for it. I meet a collector/dealer fellow who is into vintage anything (we met in the store) and he tells me how he has offered many dollars for it. No deal.

Well, Destiny beamed upon me for no apparent reason two weeks ago. I went in to check out the dresses and the Plamp was **for sale**. !!!!!!!!

They had a new "permanent fixture" in the installation, one I guessed they liked better and the Plamp stood broken and neglected, but **for sale**. The tag **now** read "Funky Lamp, As Is." Those evil words "as is." The switch was busted and after much clumsy fumbling to plug it in under a rack of Brady gowns, it failed to light and I knew why it was for sale...

Still...I bought it, after proudly maneuvering through the store, accompanied by the oohs and ahhs of stunned patrons. I drove it oh-so-carefully home, stopping on the way to get more rainbow-colored gravel from the pet supply store. There were only a few pebbles of it left in the bases and whether original or not, I decided it was a nice idea.

I got it home and my roommate, **Allan**, warmed to it after I made clear my distress that it wouldn't light. "Oh, it's just wiring. I can wire **anything**." (Yes!).

And so, the next night, we carefully undid it **all**. I soaked the "pods" in 409, detached and washed the fronds in the tub, carefully wrestled the stems and lamp-stems out of the plaster pot and cleaned everything thoroughly. The plug was found to be defective, as someone had crudely replaced it once to shorten to cord. Allan worked magic, cutting and pruning the old wires and putting new wire-nuts on.

It was time to re-attach the pods, pour gravel into the pot and put in the obligatory lo-watt non-pod-melting bulbs. Then I turned it on.

Oh. Ecstasy. It was GORGEOUS. And Allan suddenly **really liked** it. We both thought the globes would be a drab dirty-butterscotch color, but they are **MULTICOLORED, BRIGHT** and **STUNNING**.

Now it stands in our new den. It defies being ignored by guests who enter and encounter it. They either love it or hate it.

However, I am really at odds trying to explain it. Like, why was it made? Who owned it and why? (A) Restaurant or institution? (B) Custom piece for a bad Las Vegas theme lounge? (C) Home decor? That tacky sort of "Man vs. Nature" stuff again like butterflies trapped in Lucite or shower door glass? Like "Oh, let's make a far-out futuristic light, but soften the harshness of all that nasty plastic by putting some greenery around it?" Never mind that the greenery is plastic too...

At any rate, though I was vying for the Plamp, I wasn't **obsessed** with it. I had really accepted that it would either never be for sale or I would walk in and it would be inexplicably absent. But for whatever glorious reason, I walked in a mere ten days after it had been marked. Perhaps others thought it was too expensive given it was "as is" or they simply didn't notice. There were times where I never really bothered to look for a price on it, I was so used to that damn Not-For-Sale tag. I don't think I'll start collecting them as they are so big and awkward, not to mention sort of rare. Plus they're kinda bad! It's fascinating, they quickly both **heighten and drain** elegance in a setting.

Photo by Paul in AZ

By Paul Wilson, from Al Hoff's THRIFT SCORE #9

Paul Wilson, Plamp owner and artist extraordinare, montages himself dressed as "various `50s family members." That's him, on the left, as both Dick and Dottie Kimble enjoying cocktails by their Plamp. Above: "Dottie at some big touristy-thing."

neat clubs to join

United by a common interest or goal, these folks have set up bountiful emporiums of information, ideas and bumperstickers. So why not find one you like and join? Touch the meaning of brothahood.

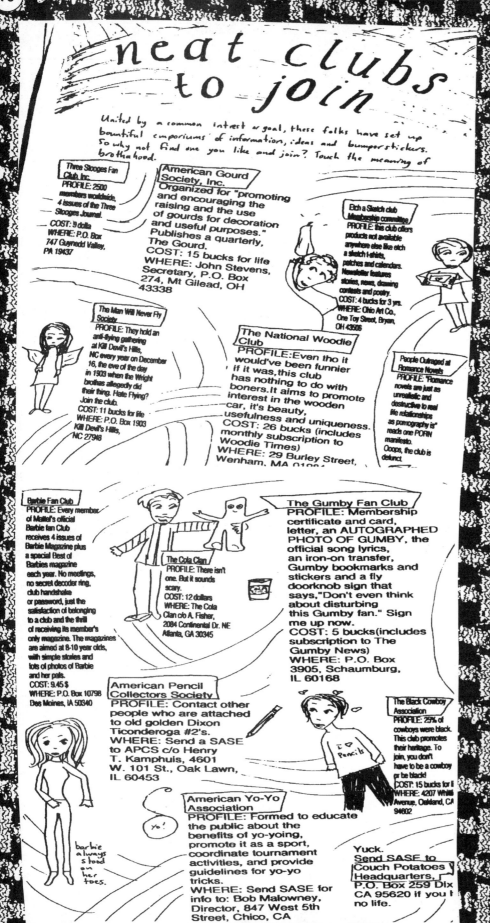

Three Stooges Fan Club, Inc.
PROFILE: 2500 members worldwide, 4 issues of the Three Stooges Journal.
COST: 9 dolla
WHERE: P.O. Box 747 Guynedd Valley, PA 19437

American Gourd Society, Inc.
Organized for "promoting and encouraging the raising and the use of gourds for decoration and useful purposes." Publishes a quarterly, The Gourd.
COST: 15 bucks for life
WHERE: John Stevens, Secretary, P.O. Box 274, Mt Gilead, OH 43338

Etch a Sketch club Membership committee
PROFILE: this club offers products not available anywhere else like etch a sketch t-shirts, patches and calendars. Newsletter features stories, news, drawing contests and poetry.
COST: 4 bucks for 3 yrs.
WHERE: Ohio Art Co., One Toy Street, Bryan, OH 43506

The Man Will Never Fly Society
PROFILE: They hold an anti-flying gathering at Kill Devil's Hills, NC every year on December 16, the eve of the day in 1903 when the Wright brothas allegedly did their thing. Hate Flying? Join the club.
COST: 11 bucks for life
WHERE: P.O. Box 1903 Kill Devil's Hills, NC 27948

The National Woodie Club
PROFILE:Even tho it would've been funnier if it was,this club has nothing to do with boners.It aims to promote interest in the wooden car, it's beauty, usefulness and uniqueness.
COST: 26 bucks (includes monthly subscription to Woodie Times)
WHERE: 29 Burley Street, Wenham, MA 0198…

People Outraged at Romance Novels
PROFILE: "Romance novels are just as unrealistic and destructive to real life relationships as pornography is" reads one PORN manifesto. Ooops, the club is defunct.

Barbie Fan Club
PROFILE: Every member of Mattel's official Barbie fan Club receives 4 issues of Barbie Magazine plus a special Best of Barbies magazine each year. No meetings, no secret decoder ring, club handshake or password, just the satisfaction of belonging to a club and the thrill of receiving its member's only magazine. The magazines are aimed at 8-10 year olds, with simple stories and lots of photos of Barbie and her pals.
COST: 9.45 $
WHERE: P.O. Box 10798 Des Moines, IA 50340

The Cola Clan
PROFILE: There isn't one. But it sounds scary.
COST: 12 dollars
WHERE: The Cola Clan c/o A. Fisher, 2084 Continental Dr. NE Atlanta, GA 30345

The Gumby Fan Club
PROFILE: Membership certificate and card, letter, an AUTOGRAPHED PHOTO OF GUMBY, the official song lyrics, an iron-on transfer, Gumby bookmarks and stickers and a fly doorknob sign that says,"Don't even think about disturbing this Gumby fan." Sign me up now.
COST: 5 bucks(includes subscription to The Gumby News)
WHERE: P.O. Box 3905, Schaumburg, IL 60168

American Pencil Collectors Society
PROFILE: Contact other people who are attached to old golden Dixon Ticonderoga #2's.
WHERE: Send a SASE to APCS c/o Henry T. Kamphuis, 4601 W. 101 St., Oak Lawn, IL 60453

The Black Cowboy Association
PROFILE: 25% of cowboys were black. This club promotes their heritage. To join, you don't have to be a cowboy or be black!
COST: 15 bucks for li…
WHERE: 4207 Whi… Avenue, Oakland, CA 94602

I ♡ Pencils

American Yo-Yo Association
PROFILE: Formed to educate the public about the benefits of yo-yoing, promote it as a sport, coordinate tournament activities, and provide guidelines for yo-yo tricks.
WHERE: Send SASE for info to: Bob Malowney, Director, 847 West 5th Street, Chico, CA

yo!

barbie always stood on her toes.

Yuck.
Send SASE to **Couch Potatoes Headquarters,** P.O. Box 259 Dix… CA 95620 if you h… no life.

THE FLABBY ARMS #7

Spry line drawings of elfin girls are a trademark of THE FLABBY ARMS, by 16-year-old Molly Aviva Brodak. "I decided to write about positive things ONLY, because there is so much snottiness and hate in the world. I wanted an optimistic zine that wasn't preachy."

CHINESE BIRTH-CONTROL POSTER

* "REMEMBER, WON TON SPELLED BACKWARDS IS... NOT NOW."

Greg Leichner is a 50-year-old writer/cartoonist and part-time carpenter who began THE POODLE-FREE NEWSLETTER as a vehicle for his "run for presidency." A rugged-looking maverick, Greg is inspired by his "loathing of the 9 to 5 American lockstep and . . . love of the free-wheeling life with lots of highway driving (three to four books-on-tape per day) and much change of venue (New Mexico, Texas, Tennessee, Ohio, Montana, Washington)."
Greg has self-published a collection of his essays and cartoons called "MAN ALIVE."

KOAN du jour

WHAT IS THE SOUND OF ONE MAN CRACKING?

KOAN du jour

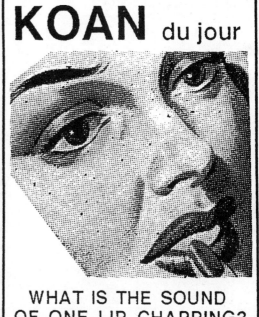

WHAT IS THE SOUND OF ONE LIP CHAPPING?

by Greg Leichner, POODLE-FREE NEWSLETTER

OUTROS

Now that you've unearthed all the raw gems of your consciousness and shared them, you might consider polishing 'em up with an OUTRO. These are usually brief goodbyes that can also express appreciation to those who helped bring your zine to light.

If there's a point you want to emphasize, the outro is the place to do it. It's also your last chance to include the vitals: info about how to order your zine, how much it costs, if back issues are available, etc.

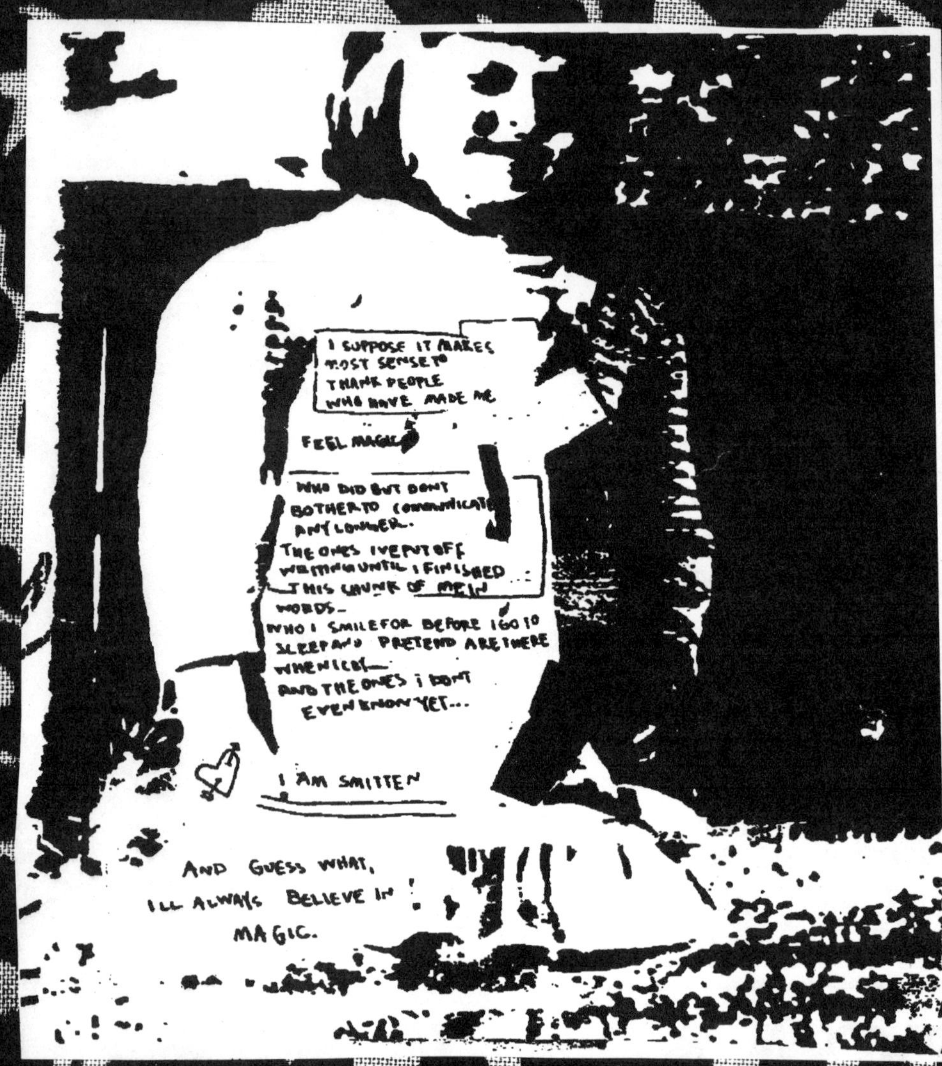

Gretchen Christina Lowther, GOOD FAERIE #12 1/2

We hope that some of these *zinelements* will ignite your creative spirit, but don't get stuck here! Like Emily K. Larned, MUFFIN BONES, sez:

> ". . . don't be afraid to be wholly original. This may seem like a banal statement, but unfortunately many editors must have this fear because too many zines today have a standard sort of 'zine fare,' menu, you know, rants, reviews, interviews, and collages. Yawn. This sounds horribly cruel but I don't mean to be cruel, it's just that I know that I felt safe when I had generic zine contents, and when I look back on those issues, I realize safety is boring."

ZINE GERALDINE OR ZINE EUGENE?

PICKING A NAME

Now that you know what's in your zine, what do you call it? A great zine name is one of the best ways to draw your reader to you. Some people believe that if you know someone's true name you know their soul and can have power over them. Have you ever noticed that when someone uses your name in a conversation, it can affect you emotionally? Like when your mom uses your full name when she is mad at you, your love uses it when you are making out, or it's typed into a sweepstakes letter:

PEACHY McGEE, congratulations! Your awesome zine has been selected to be featured in ZINE SCENE! Just sign the enclosed form and you, **PEACHY McGEE**, will be eligible for many fabulous prizes! MORE PEN PALS! HIGHER DISTRO! UNSURPASSED EXCITEMENT!

You get the point. Names are potent. Choosing a kid's name is pretty important; certain names can bring with them a lifetime of teasing. With zines, however, the tease factor is usually a plus. It's hard to forget names such as SATAN WEARS A BRA or J. CRUELTY CATALOGUE!

How did some zinesters come up with their names? Tamra Spivey found her title, ERACISM, written in chalk on an old univox amp head she bought from a friend.

Tamra Spivey (who lists her age as "ageism cuts both ways"), is the creator of LUCID NATION, tvi, and ERACISM, as well as an active presence in the zine community.
Her zines have been used by doctoral candidates in Orange County, California, and are also read in Poland, Guam, and Spain. "*tvi* made it to mtv, which is pretty funny because it cuts mtv so bad."

EVENTUALLY, I NEEDED TO COME UP WITH A NAME FOR MY COMIC BOOK. THE CATBOX WAS SITUATED UNDER MY DRAWING TABLE, AND I ENDED UP USING IT AS A FOOTREST WHENEVER I SAT AT MY DESK. I REALIZED MY BEDROOM HAD BECOME THE CATBOX ROOM. THE TITLE NOT ONLY FIT MY BEDROOM, BUT ALSO MY LIFE, MY BRAIN, AND MY COMIC BOOK.
SIX MONTHS AGO, I MOVED OUT OF MASONIC YOUTH HOSTEL. HAIGHT STREET AND THE NEIGHBORING CRACK HOUSE HAD BECOME QUITE TIRESOME AFTER THREE AND A HALF YEARS. NOW I LIVE IN A FLAT ON D. STREET. IT'S NEAR HAIGHT STREET BUT THE NEIGHBORHOOD IS MUCH LESS SHITTY. MY CATS ARE VERY HAPPY HERE BECAUSE THERE'S MORE SPACE, STAIRS, GOOD WINDOWS, AND COOL SPOTS FOR THEM TO CHILL. WHEN WE MOVED IN, I TRIED TO PUT THE CATBOX IN THE BATHROOM, BUT IT DIDN'T FLY WITH MY ROOMMATES. SO GUESS WHAT. I STILL LIVE IN THE CATBOX ROOM. BUT TO TELL YOU THE TRUTH, THAT'S JUST FINE WITH ME.
LM'94

Lisa Maslowe, THE CATBOX ROOM #2

NAME THAT ZINE

Michael, CULTURE FREAK: "The title for my zine comes from a mail order bride catalog. A Swedish woman named Katarina stated in her mildly broken English, 'I consider myself an intellectual, but try to avoid culture-freak.'"

Stephanie Kuehnert, HOSPITAL GOWN: ". . . because I'm making myself vulnerable. This is called hospital gown because I'm flashing my ass at you and daring you to kick it . . . because I'm ripping out the IVs he used to feed me. I am kicking and screaming, refusing to be sedated. I want my clothes back. Naked as I am, I refuse to be violated again."

Marissa Walsh, age 24, INDIGNANT GINGHAM: "I have been known to be indignant. I have also been known to wear gingham."

Lorena Melgoza, age 20, U.G.L.Y., MIRAME: "The name UGLY (Unite Girls Love Yourself) and what it stands for seriously just came to me like that—in a flash. MIRAME (Spanish for 'Look at me') to me sounds assertive, fearless, honest, like a dare—'Yeah, look at me! Mirame!'"

Tai, CICADA: ". . . just because of what they are. Little things that lie dormant for 17 years then suddenly come out, seemingly from nowhere, and start making NOISE."

Brain Ralph, FIREBALL: "From this cat that lived next door—he was a nice cat and I think his name was Fireball. But now that I think about it, it might have been Snowball."

Erin McClarley, age 17, GLAMOUR QUEEN: ". . . i'm not a glamour queen according to miss america standards, nor do i want to be, but i am a glamour queen cos i set my own standards that are realistic and rad."

Thomas, ONE QUIET VOICE: "I got the name from a song by Fidelity Jones called, 'Bloodstone Burn.' There's this one line that goes, 'In the clamor of vaunting and hatred and pride/One Quiet Voice is driven out.' I thought that that line fit me to a tee . . . I'm solitary and quiet and this zine is my voice."

Tim Stocoak's zine, BEA & EFF, was named after two old friends of his grandmother's who worked in the ink and paint department at Hanna-Barbera in the '60s. Robert Northrup came up with DELINQUENT WENCH as "revenge" when Debbie, his pen-pal of five years, suddenly and inexplicably stopped writing to him.

There are lots of ways for you to think of titles. Maybe you can find the name of your zine by playing some:

ZINE SCENE NAME-GAMES!

1. Make three columns of your fave words and pick one from each column.

lobster	chiromancy	bumbershoot
birthday	mocha	antics
luminous	gingivitis	snit
volcanic	devoted	jade

How about a zine called VOLCANIC GINGIVITIS ANTICS? Or just pick two: LUMINOUS SNIT.

2. This is a game for finding your **zine alias**:

Combine the name of your childhood pet with your mother's maiden name.

Hillary is "Monkey Leiverman"

Francesca is "Coco Klein"

You can use these names as zine titles, too.

3. Why not take a word and make an anagram of it? In fact, there's a very cool Web site online that automatically does it for you! (**http://www.infobahn.com/pages/anagram.html/**). Our names scrambled into some surprising zine title possibilities:

Hillary Sue Carlip: Purely Lilac Hairs; Hail, Surly Replica; Peculiar Lily Rash.

Francesca Lia Block: Fancies Black Coral; Conceals Frail Back; Africa Beckons Call.

4. Another cool way to find a name is to look at signs and graffiti around you. Why not name a zine from a found object like the following lost pet poster? A possible zine title: DISTINGUISHING FEATURES: BREATH.

MORE NAME THAT ZINE

Sara McCool, age 19, SOURPUSS: "I had a dream in which someone just kept yelling sourpuss over and over again at me, and when I woke up and was remembering my dream I was like hey, that sounds like a good name for a zine."

Jim Freek, age 28, FRUITBASKET UPSET: ". . . is the title of an unreleased Archies song."

Edan Lepucki and Vanessa Dingivan, CROATAN: ". . .' Sir Walter Raleigh set up the first colony in America . . . he left for three years, and when he returned he found that his entire settlement had vanished. The only sign that humans had been there was the word *croatan* etched into a tree. We thought that this was mystifying and makes you wonder . . . how we want our zine to be."

Christian Merry, BLACK VIRGIN MARY COLORING BOOK: "The Black Virgin Mary Icon was what all the czar and czarinas prayed to when they wanted to accomplish something big . . . they and many other cultures knew no virginal white goody goody was going to get out there and help them cut heads off and partition countries like cake. I would rather acknowledge the passionate side of being a human, not the unrealistic world of 'Fear Of' sex and smell and eating with your hands, and thinking not just accepting . . . So the babe for the job in some circles is The Black Virgin Mary. Either that or it just sounded so good in front of 'Coloring Book.' "

ZINE TEAM

ALONE...

You may choose to write a zine that is strictly by and about you. MUFFIN BONES, for example, makes no bones about it: "no submissions please!" This is great if you want your zine to maintain a distinct vision and tone.

It's a blissfully personal experience to write a solo zine, and reading one is like getting a letter from a friend or snooping (without the guilt) into someone's diary. Some solos can have a great deal of variety, too, if the zinester in question is graphically stylin' and writes about eclectic subjects.

... OR TOGETHER

Another way to do a zine is to use the above approach, but add a few contributions from your readers or pals in the form of comix, poetry, or even letters to the editor/editrix.

This approach lets you maintain your overall concept but makes people feel included and adds some spice-of-life. Because your contributors and their friends will probably want copies, it could even expand your readership.

Be resourceful in finding contributors. Jim Freek of FRUITBASKET UPSET includes a piece in each issue from Echo, "our 10-year-old neighbor girl who scribbles her thoughts in the name of punk rock, Melrose Place, and elementary school."

Tamra Spivey of LUCID NATION, tvi, and ERACISM zines, reprinted a transcript of a chat she instigated online regarding the "musical question of the decade" in which Courtney Love and other industry constellations participated.

In issue #6, Ceci SUBURBIA stayed a little closer to home ➡

Jesus Christ Broke into my House!

By: My Dad

I guess I had a profound religious experience but it did not registe with me until now. It was a 5:30 AM on a spring morning in Richmond, California at my home. I heard a streng knocking on my front door. Who could be visiting so early? My heart pounded and I cautiously went to see who was there. I asked the visitor who he was and what he wanted. The answer came "I'm Jesus Christ and I have come to free my people." My response- "wrong house, maybe your people are waiting for you at another home, but they are not here."

My visitor then left, so I thought. A few moments later I heard a noise on my neighbor's side deck just a few feet from a window of my house. It was "Jesus" trying to look into my home for "his people."

Very shortly thereafter Jesus was at my front door again, demanding in a strong loud voice for me to let him in.

I picked up the phone and called 911 and got a busy signal, par for the course in Richmond, California.

Jesus was getting very impatient and started kicking at the door. I called 911 again and got an answer. I told them what was happening and the operator asked if it was a "true emergency" and "was the man at the door threatening me with a weapon." I answered "no, he was just trying to kick down my front door to get in to free his people."

At this point I took my cordless phone and myself out another door and waited for the police. Meanwhile, "Jesus" kicked open the locked door and went upstairs.

The police arrived about 20 minutes later. In the meantime the neighbors on each side of me are aware of "Jesus" finding my home and we all waited out front for the police.

The police arrived and asked "Jesus" to come out. No response. 3 cops enter through the broken doorway and call again. No response. They proceed up the stairs and find "Jesus" preaching to his people. "The people" apparently were living in my house disguised as firewood logs next to the hearth. "Jesus" had removed the logs and carefully line them up in the living room and was preaching to his just freed people.

The 3 cops could not pull down "Jesus" as he had god like super strength so more cops were brought in to assist. Finally, Jesus was dragged out and sent away in a patrol car. Being "Jesus" he was not hauled off to jail but taken to the hospital psychiatric ward for observation. It turns out it was not Jesus but a guy very high on speed and psychedelics!

<<<<<<<<<<<<< The only picture I have of Jesus at the moment. (This picture makes me laugh SOOOOO hard!!!!!!! Hey, come over here hot stuff, what's your sign?? God almighty, you look cute tonight!!!!! (Like I said, I am going to hell, hands down.) Kinda looks like Fabio, huh? I never thought I'd ever make that comparison!

← Sacrilegious? Who? me?

"My dad's my best friend -- that's why he gets stuff in my zine. He's constantly telling funny stories and I need a little humor to lighten things up in my zine. For those like my dad who don't have access, time, or energy to do their own zine, it's a good idea to grant space for them. It adds another interesting dimension. It can get kinda boring to read just one person's POV.."

- Ceci Suburbia

But be aware: If you open up your zine to contributors, you might not always get what you want.

"There's no room in my zine for a comic strip about the cutesy work-a-day world of Arnie the Animating Armadillo. People actually send me this stuff! It's disheartening to me—these folks seem to like my zine but I can see they don't 'get it' when they send me this crap. Printing that sort of material in my zine would be like running that comic strip 'Love Is...' in *Penthouse*."

- Tim Stocoak, BEA & EFF

Finally, there's the team-zine. This has advantages and disadvantages.

ADVANTAGES OF THE ZINE-TEAM THING:

1. While you're addressing envelopes, you can talk with your collaborator about your crushy encounter with that pup-boy or kitty-girl.

2. You can get it done faster with more than one zinester.

3. You can add variety to your zine by including the work of other *zine-iuses.*

4. It's fun to share the triumph . . .

5. . . . And it helps to have someone around when stuff doesn't go the way you planned!

DISADVANTAGES OF THE ZINE TEAM THING:

If you choose a team, look for, if not soulmates, than at least like-minded collaborators. It's great to have different opinions and views, for variety's sake, but you should be able to agree on certain basics. Who has final say on what's included in the zine? Is it one person or are decisions equally divided? If you decide together, it's especially important to want the same things from the zine experience.

Also, you may be spending a lot of hours with these cats and chix so make sure you like their company. It's a very hot thing to read a zine by more than one zinemaniac when they are really in tune with each other. The chemistry is palpable, which increases the enjoyment of the reading experience.

ZINE SCENE

WHERE DO YOU CREATE YOUR MASTERPIECE?

Francesca has a cloud pink room with windows looking out over some eucalyptus trees.[1] Her dog[2] usually lies next to her, batting his long eyelashes. There is an altar with a statue of Aphrodite,[3] a piece of rose quartz, a genie[4] incense burner, and globe lamp. There is a case with, among other books, *Nine Stories* by J.D. Salinger, *To the Lighthouse* by Virginia Woolf, and *The Fairy Tradition In Britain* by Lewis Spence.[5]

Hillary works at a window surrounded by trees and the Hollywood sign.[6] The sill is lined with statues of Mary and saints (Teresa of Avila[7] and Clair, Patroness of television). A high shelf goes around the whole office displaying a dazzling collection of '50s pulp paperbacks[8] (with brilliantly illustrated technicolor covers). The wall behind holds shelves of found objects for art pieces (shopping lists,[9] puppets, doll heads, pin-up girls[10]) and to the left is a large bookcase full of notebooks, journals, scripts, and scraps. On the desk (besides the necessities) are candles, sage smudge, and a desk nameplate found at a flea market in Rome.[11]

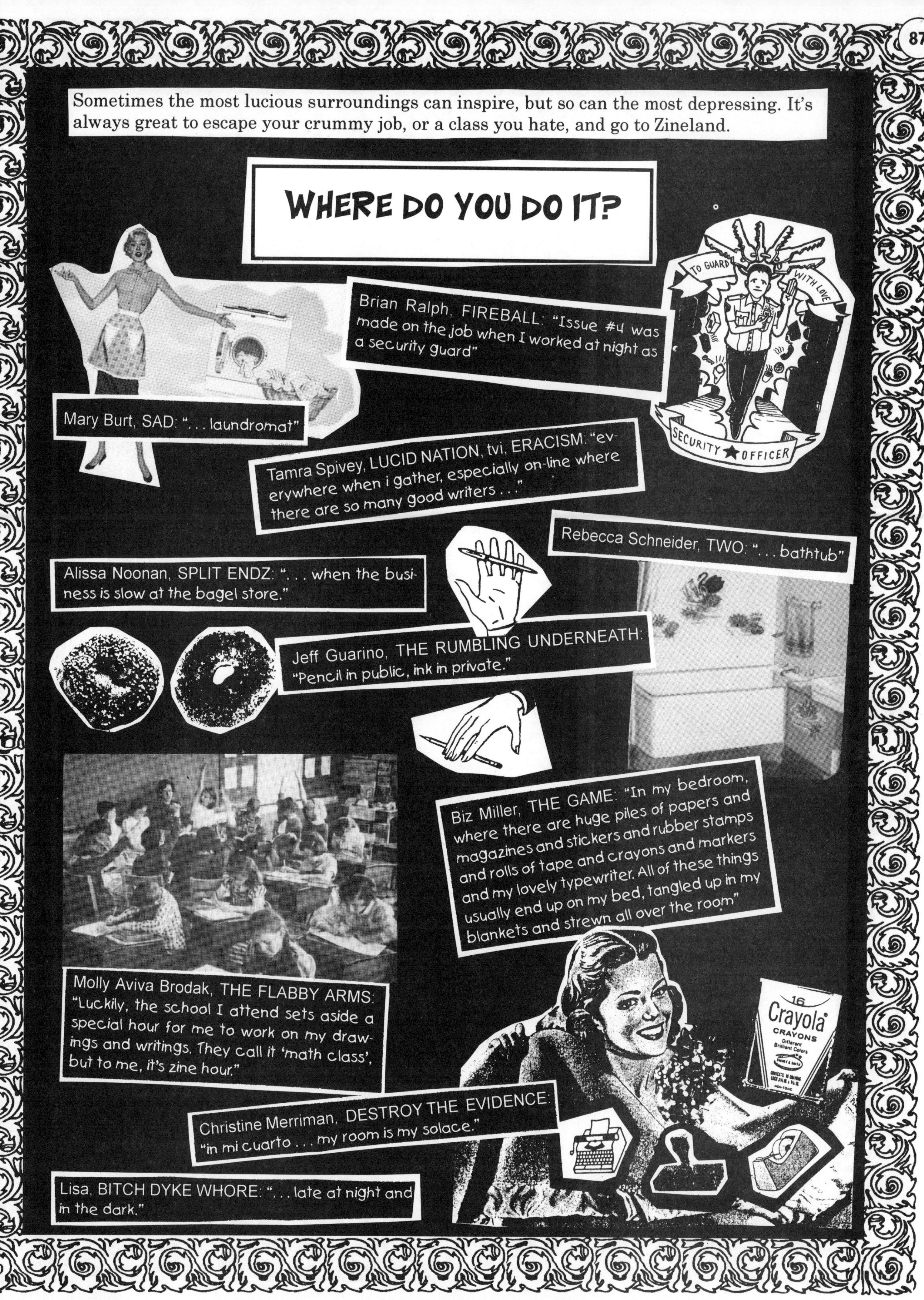

Sometimes the most lucious surroundings can inspire, but so can the most depressing. It's always great to escape your crummy job, or a class you hate, and go to Zineland.

WHERE DO YOU DO IT?

Brian Ralph, FIREBALL: "Issue #4 was made on the job when I worked at night as a security guard"

Mary Burt, SAD: ". . . laundromat"

Tamra Spivey, LUCID NATION, tvi, ERACISM: "everywhere when i gather, especially on-line where there are so many good writers . . ."

Rebecca Schneider, TWO: ". . . bathtub"

Alissa Noonan, SPLIT ENDZ: ". . . when the business is slow at the bagel store."

Jeff Guarino, THE RUMBLING UNDERNEATH: "Pencil in public, ink in private."

Biz Miller, THE GAME: "In my bedroom, where there are huge piles of papers and magazines and stickers and rubber stamps and rolls of tape and crayons and markers and my lovely typewriter. All of these things usually end up on my bed, tangled up in my blankets and strewn all over the room"

Molly Aviva Brodak, THE FLABBY ARMS: "Luckily, the school I attend sets aside a special hour for me to work on my drawings and writings. They call it 'math class', but to me, it's zine hour."

Christine Merriman, DESTROY THE EVIDENCE: "in mi cuarto . . . my room is my solace."

Lisa, BITCH DYKE WHORE: ". . . late at night and in the dark."

ZINE SHEEN

GETTING YOUR LOOK

Now that you know what's going to be in your zine, how do you present it?

One of the first choices you get to make is whether to write it by hand or type it (or include some of both.) This will greatly depend on what you have available to you.

Don't get stuck thinking, "I don't have a typewriter or computer so I can't do it *that* way." Computers are available for public use where you'd least expect it: Cafes, libraries, schools, and copy shops. (Watch out for copy shops. They can be pricy!)

If you are going to handwrite some or all of your zine, be sure to be aware of:

LEGIBILITY

Who knows what Baroque pearls and sizzling diamonds of content lie buried in the impossibly small print, or floppity-sloppity-scrawly handwriting of a rough-to-read zine?

It might seem punk rock to be illegible but if you want to get your message out to more people than just yourself, you might consider printing with care, investing in a typewriter, upping the font size on your computer, or asking a friend to help.

DESIGN

Use photos, illustrations, and artwork done by you or by someone who has given you permission to include their work. You can separate the image from your text like Mariah McDougall does in REWM:

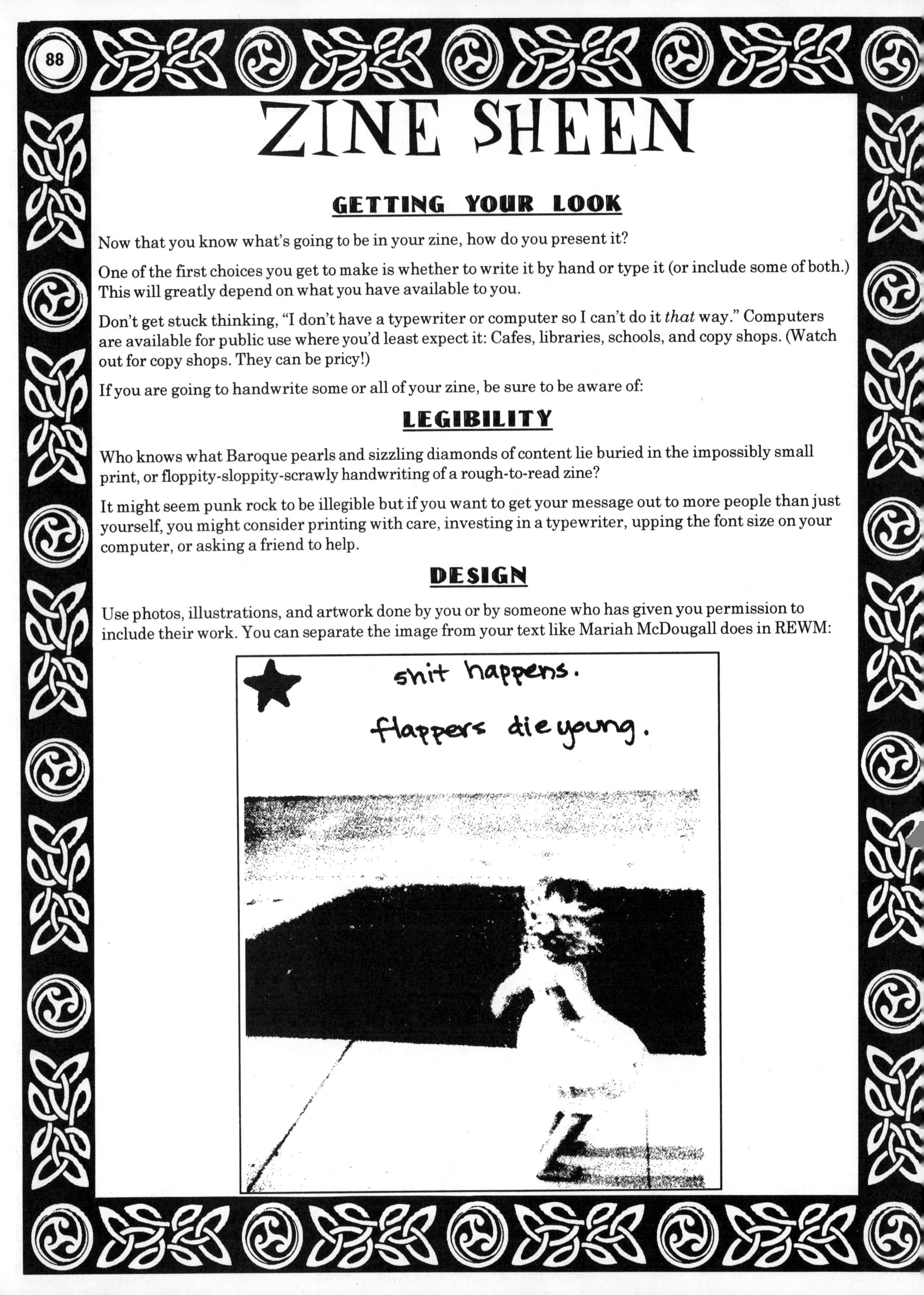

Or you can put text *over* the image á la Jessika Farris in REJECT GENE:

Two girls are helping each other with a home permanent. One girl wants
to cut off her long hair. The other doesn't want her to and attempts to keep her
rom it.
Two girls are staying all night with each other. One is on a diet and is
letermined not to snack between meals. The other is snacking and tries to get her
friend to do likewise.
A girl is at a party and a boy attempts to make friends with her. She doesn't think
she should accept a date with him because she has just met him. He is
determined to get a date with her.
Two cheer leaders are working out a yell routine. One wants to jump in the air
after each yell. The other insists they should bow with their pompoms in front of
them at the end of each routine.
WOMB WOMB DREAM
DANGER

Why not make your own collages such as SWEETHEART Robin Crane's beauties?

Some zines include pieces drawn by the zinester like Christian Merry's art in the BLACK VIRGIN MARY COLORING BOOK:

Other zines, like THE STEVEN LIEBER SKETCHBOOK MINI, are *all* drawings:

(This big stone Buddha) "was drawn from life on a hillside in Hong Kong. It was raining, and I had to hunch over my sketchbook to keep it from getting soaked. A Japanese tourist leaned over to see what I was doing, and when she saw the trouble I was having with the rain, moved her umbrella to cover me and stayed there until I finished."

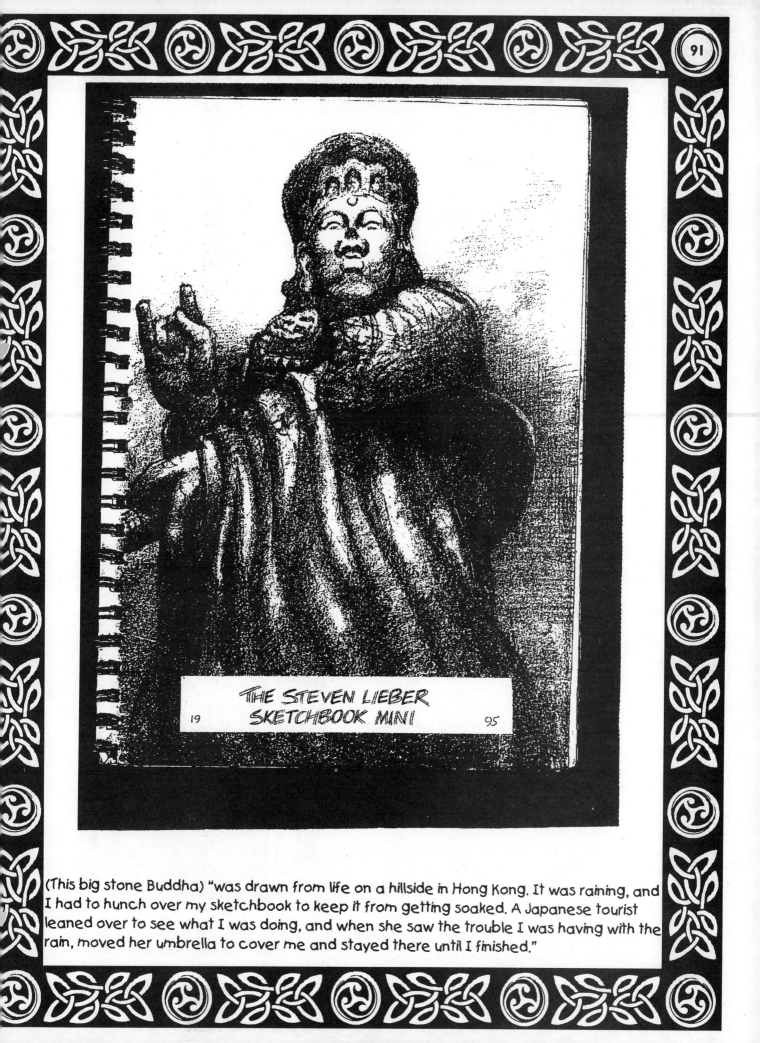

COPYRIGHT

If you do use someone else's artwork (or writing, for that matter) it's good *zinetiquette* to get permission, and then acknowledge the author/artist for their contributions. Give credit where credit's due.

Zines are notorious for including whatever the zinester pleases, but there are potential copyright problems if you use something without permission and your zine gets into a lot of hands. One zinester had to stop using the title HEY THERE, BARBIE when Mattel, the company which makes the legendary doll, threatened to take legal action. Another zine, BUNNYHOP, parodied a character by "The Simpsons" cartoonist Matt Groening. The zinester was forced to destroy all the copies printed. Also, since Kinko's Copy Center lost a lot of money in a lawsuit for reproducing copyright-protected material without authors' permission, they are now incredibly selective about what they will and will not photocopy for their customers.

CLIP ART

But do not fret—there's always clip art. You can just cut out and use these copyright-free images. There are some cool clip art books (eg. "MOSTLY HAPPY! CLIP ART OF THE THIRTIES, FORTIES AND FIFTIES" selected and edited by Jerry Jankowski, published by Art Direction Book Co.) Most clip art images are fairly standard, and not racially diverse. Robyn E. Lee, of GIRL DETECTIVE, says, "Research your ass off for clip art. The coolest stuff can be found on your grocery bag! Save everything! I find myself getting inspired for a whole article, just to use a really cool piece of clip art." Make sure the image or written piece is copyright-free.

Simply cut and paste. It's that cut and dry. Experiment. If you're doing your layout by hand, see what glue tickles your fancy. Some zinesters prefer *rubber cement*—it doesn't dry right away and you can move things around. The same with *spray adhesive*— which also doesn't curl or crinkle the paper. How about *two-sided tape*? Be sure all edges of your image are down firmly so paste-up lines don't show when you photocopy. And there's always that grammar school favorite: *the glue stick*.

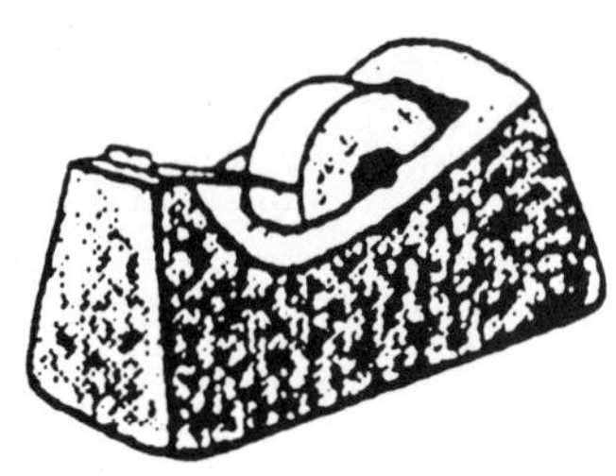

Use your imagination for backgrounds. Why not borrow a placemat? Or a piece of fabric? Several of the backgrounds in this book were photocopied from shirts. Raid your closet!

How about experimenting with other unique ways of lettering, like Jose Torres does in SELLOUT BOY?

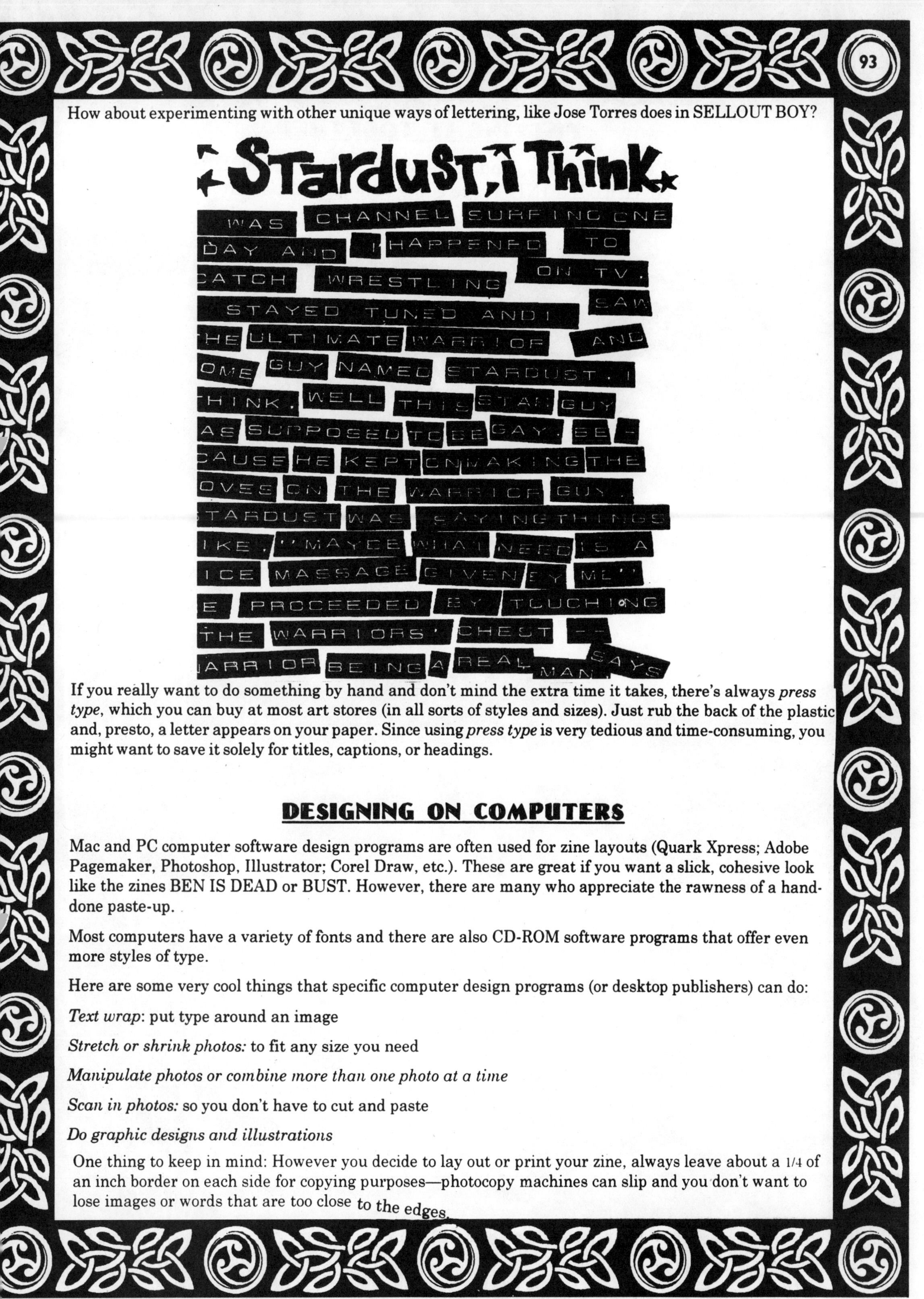

If you really want to do something by hand and don't mind the extra time it takes, there's always *press type*, which you can buy at most art stores (in all sorts of styles and sizes). Just rub the back of the plastic and, presto, a letter appears on your paper. Since using *press type* is very tedious and time-consuming, you might want to save it solely for titles, captions, or headings.

DESIGNING ON COMPUTERS

Mac and PC computer software design programs are often used for zine layouts (Quark Xpress; Adobe Pagemaker, Photoshop, Illustrator; Corel Draw, etc.). These are great if you want a slick, cohesive look like the zines BEN IS DEAD or BUST. However, there are many who appreciate the rawness of a hand-done paste-up.

Most computers have a variety of fonts and there are also CD-ROM software programs that offer even more styles of type.

Here are some very cool things that specific computer design programs (or desktop publishers) can do:

Text wrap: put type around an image

Stretch or shrink photos: to fit any size you need

Manipulate photos or combine more than one photo at a time

Scan in photos: so you don't have to cut and paste

Do graphic designs and illustrations

One thing to keep in mind: However you decide to lay out or print your zine, always leave about a 1/4 of an inch border on each side for copying purposes—photocopy machines can slip and you don't want to lose images or words that are too close to the edges.

PUTTING IT TOGETHER

Zines come in all shapes, colors, and sizes. Sara McCool, of SOURPUSS, and Emilie Feingold-Tarrant of GIRL INFINITY, are going to help us illustrate some of the different layout options for printing.

SIZE:

The easiest way is to start with a **standard** letter-size piece of paper—8 1/2" x 11". Your zine could be this size and printed on both sides of the paper. Or you could print just one side and staple it up in the corner—which is easier, but less economical.

One of the most common zine sizes is the standard letter-size page, FOLDED IN HALF to 8 1/2" x 5 1/2" . We'll call it **half-standard.**

The half-standard layout is kind of tricky since both sides of the paper will be photocopied, so make sure you've gotten enough sleep, or have had a huge glass o' Jolt Cola or something, before you read ahead.

Let's say you're doing a **ten-page, half-standard sized zine**. It will actually be twelve pages, including the front and back cover.

You can lay it out so you'll use just three pieces of paper:

1.

back cover	front cover

flip it over to your right and on the back you'll have......

pg. 1	pg. 10

2.

pg. 9	pg. 2

flip it over to your right and on the back you'll have......

pg. 3	pg. 8

3.

pg. 7	pg. 4

flip it over to your right and on the back you'll have......

pg. 5	pg. 6

Put #1, 2, and 3 in order, and you're ready to print. It's a good idea to include page numbers on your zine. This will help you put it all together after you've made a bunch of copies.

The above demonstration can be applied to a half-size smaller, also referred to as **quarter size** (5 1/2" x 4 1/4"), so you can actually paste up *four* pages on each side of standard paper!

4 pages on one side →

size ← when cut and folded

These configurations can be done with a **legal-size** piece of paper as well. Either 8 1/2" x 14". . .

. . . Or the above size folded in half: 8 1/2" x 7"; or in quarters; 4 1/4" x 7". And don't forget the largest size paper that most copiers will take: 11" x 17". This size can be folded in half to 8 1/2" x 11" and then again, to 8 1/2" x 5 1/2" so you can lay out 8 pages per sheet (4 double-sided pages)! It'll end up being the same size as the half-standard.

Another option is to take the 11" x 17" paper and paste up 12 sections per sheet (6 double-sided pages). Your zine will wind up being 5 1/2" x 5 2/3" .

Of course you can experiment with other sizes. Strange things have crossed our very crowded ZINE SCENE desks like the 4 1/4" x 14" pictured below:

Keep in mind that you'll have an even amount of pages, so make sure you have something to put on them all.

You'll need to paste up each page knowing exactly what size it will be.

Experiment radly with the layout of your zine. To read MY EVIL TWIN SISTER, you have to chop off the top margin and separate the pages. SMELLY CAT is printed on sticker paper.

And speaking of printing . . .

COPY CATS AND CHIX

Most zines are photocopied. Others are done by *offset printing* which can look more professional, and usually cleaner. Although it's ultimately cheaper per copy to offset, there's usually a minimum number of copies you must make, which demands a greater cash output. Either way, the more copies you make, the cheaper it is per page.

Both offset and photocopying can be done on white or colored paper (or something like the swirly marbleized stuff Janice Headly uses for her COPACETIC covers) and offset can be done on newsprint as well. With offset printing, photographs can be *half-toned* which reproduces a lot of the details more clearly. While some of the newer photocopying machines have a half-tone setting, the image usually comes out looking dotty and gray and you might prefer a basic setting which provides more black and white contrast. Colored inks can be used with either photocopying or offset printing.

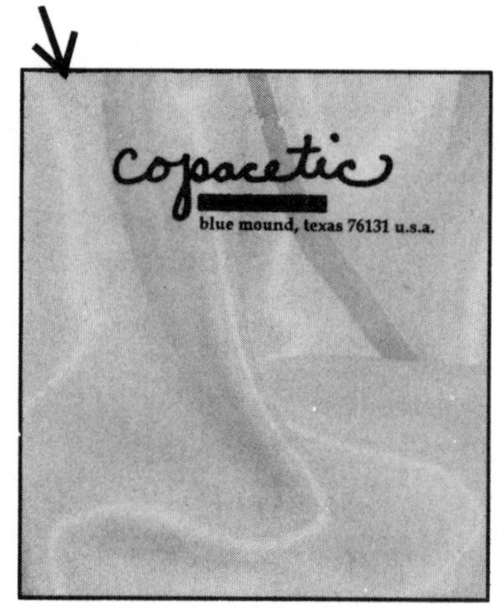

There's always color copying like Elizabeth used for the cover of SHERA (FREEDOM SLUT) #1, but that can get extremely costly. You might want to try some hand-coloring—whip out those pens, pencils, crayons, and paints after you've copied.

Be creative in finding printing resources. Abraham Katzman of FLAMING JEWBOY and I'M OVER BEING DEAD gets "help" from a "Friend at a chain copy shop that rhymes with Ginko's."

ASSEMBLY LINE

Ready to put together your zine? If you've copied more than one page per paste-up sheet, you can cut them apart by hand or with a paper cutter. To bind, think practically *and* creatively. Fold, then either staple down the side (two staples facing in), or use a rubber band, pipe cleaner, piece of yarn—anything that holds the pages together without them getting unruly and unwieldy. If you are planning to make more than a handful of issues, you might consider going for the simplest techniques. Keep in mind that some bindings won't hold up in the mail unless they're protected by an envelope.

Michael, CULTURE FREAK

POST IT

There are many possibilities when it comes to mailing your work of wonder. As mentioned earlier, you can let the back cover act as the front of an envelope, addressing right on the zine itself. If you do that, you'll then have to either tape or staple the zine so firmly that it holds together while postal workers throw it from bin to bin to box. But keep in mind: Some zines can take as long to open as they do to read. A little goes a long way when it comes to stapling or taping your zines for mailing.

You might decide you'd rather use envelopes. They can be inventive and ecologically correct, like Mary Burt's SAD 'lope that was made from recycled troll doll Christmas wrapping paper. MAGDALENE'S Mariah McDougall took a letter-size envelope with a cellophane window and taped a pic so it peeked through. Envelopes can serve to hide a zine from prying eyes—one fan of BITCH DYKE WHORE was concerned about her parents seeing it in the mailbox—and also give you more room for your art (hand-drawn, stickers, stamps,etc.)

Another thing you'll want on your mailed zine is your return address, but remember: **ALWAYS USE A P.O. BOX. NEVER GIVE OUT YOUR HOME ADDRESS OR PHONE NUMBER!** You never know what creepsters might want to correspond. At least they won't know where you live! If you start getting mail that gives you the willies in any way (too frequent, excessively personal references, obsessive-sounding), we suggest that you don't respond. Tell your family, friends, or maybe even your local police if it gets out of hand.

Some zinesters, like Christine Merriman, DESTROY THE EVIDENCE, are mobilizing against harassment:

in most cases, i would never use somebody's name in a situation like this, but since he has used mine (along with tons of other kids) in his recent attempt to defend himself, i will do the same. although many of xthe people reading this may have k heard of ███ and what kind of stuff he pulls, a lot of you may have not either. i am not going to write a bunch of rumors right now, fif you want to hear them just ask me and i'll tell you privately. (i have to be real careful what i say, cos ███ seems to think that he xcan sue anyone who sees through him.) this man is trying to contact as many girls as possible, and will use his riot grrrl book proposal as a way to interest you. he brags about the "professional" zine he does,

subliminal tattoos, and will do his best to impress you. any of you who have yet to hear from him; please think twice about responding to his oh-so-innocent form letter. this isn't just a matter of personal disagreements; ███ has done thingsx that make me wonder why the fuck he isn't sitting in a prison cell instead fof his cozy little home in washington. he has been known to print people's quotes without permission, so if you must write him at least watch what you say and choose your words carefully. for the whole story on ███, send a donation (at least a few dollars please- this thing is huge) and get kool man. it's been edited by sean craphound and totally describes everything, although some of it may xmake you want to vomit. (sex with underage girls, cheating on his wife, the scam behind his sex zine etc.)

i'm sure this isn't the first time something like this has happened, nor will it be the last. xi just hope something positive will result from the mistakes of those of us who ever responded in the first place, and if i can convince anyone to think twice about trusting people i know it will have been worth it.

ODDEST ZINE-RELATED THING THAT'S HAPPENED

Ceci, SUBURBIA: "On my first issue I put 'free to prisoners' when I sent it to *Factsheet Five*. After the review was published, I kept getting all these letters from convicts . . . I felt sorry for them, but I was too scared to write them. I didn't know if they were child molesters or serial killers. Not that I had a choice, my dad forbade me to write back. Also, my best friend gave #4 to her little sister. Now her sister worships my zine (she's 11). She spent her summer videotaping herself reading it."

Brian Ralph, FIREBALL: ". . . seeing my comics show up in weird places. On the backs of leather jackets, tattoos, etc . . ."

Rebecca D. Dillon, VELVET GRASS: "[My zine] was presented in court as evidence against me (when I went after a rapist)."

Lorena Melgoza, U.G.L.Y.: "We received death threats and threatening messages. But we handled it all quite well. Anytime you speak out, it's a risk that you're taking. No matter what, there will always be people out there who don't like you or what you're saying and they want to shut you up. But they didn't! And they can't!"

Sara McCool, SOURPUSS: "One time I was trying to give this boy my zine and he wouldn't take it, so I got really obnoxious with him, and he said he didn't know how to read, and I was like sure I don't believe that, then he got really sad and walked away and I found out later he really didn't know how to read, so I felt like a jerk."

Dan Moynihan, MICROBLAST: "Getting a pistachio donut in the mail."

To avoid any problems of this sort, be aware, and stay connected with the zine community.

LOOK!

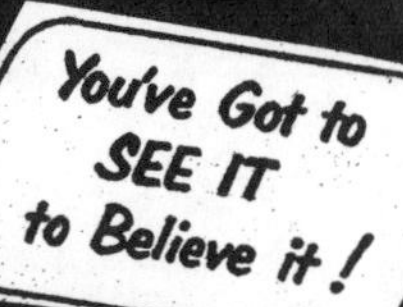
You've Got to
SEE IT
to Believe it!

"COME 'N' GET IT!"

SECTION THREE

PAY UP

RAISING $$$ TO DO YOUR ZINE

No one might ever get to see that vibrant volatile butterfly that is your soul if you can't afford to make copies of the zine that embodies it, or pay for stamps to send it off.

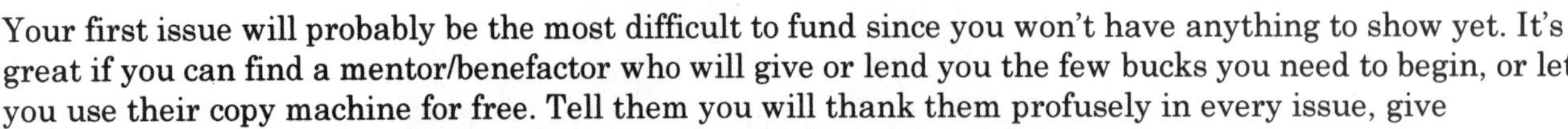

Your first issue will probably be the most difficult to fund since you won't have anything to show yet. It's great if you can find a mentor/benefactor who will give or lend you the few bucks you need to begin, or let you use their copy machine for free. Tell them you will thank them profusely in every issue, give them complimentary copies for the rest of their lives, or feature their work. If you make these offers and you are rejected, don't despair. You'll just have to rely on your own resources.

Here are some ways to raise cash for things like glue, scissors, a P.O. box, photocopying, envelopes, and stamps:

♦ **OVEN LOVE** Make some vegan banana poppyseed muffins and have a bake sale.

♦ **SHAMELESSLY SELF PROMOTE** Ask for donations from friends, family, teachers, librarians, bosses.

♦ **ROCK OUT** Get together with some friends and dance or play guitar for spare change.

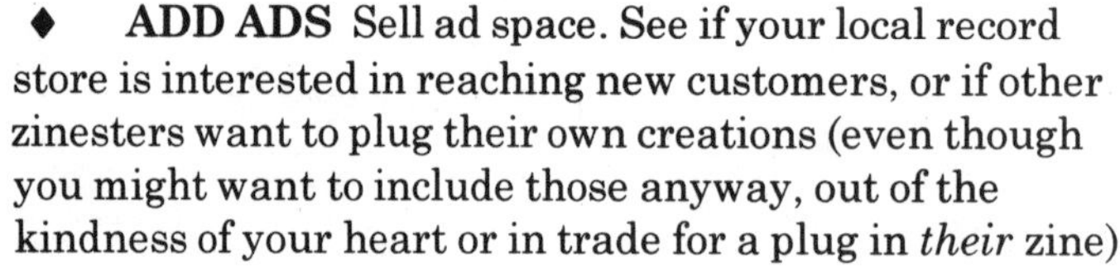

♦ **ADD ADS** Sell ad space. See if your local record store is interested in reaching new customers, or if other zinesters want to plug their own creations (even though you might want to include those anyway, out of the kindness of your heart or in trade for a plug in *their* zine).

♦ **USE YOUR HANDS** . . . MAD GIRL, Emily Anne, makes and sells T-shirts:

Emily, MUFFIN BONES, makes and sells Kitty Hats. HERO GRRRL's Jessica Wilbur sells notebooks hand-decorated with collaged pics, glitter, puffy paints, bells, and beads.

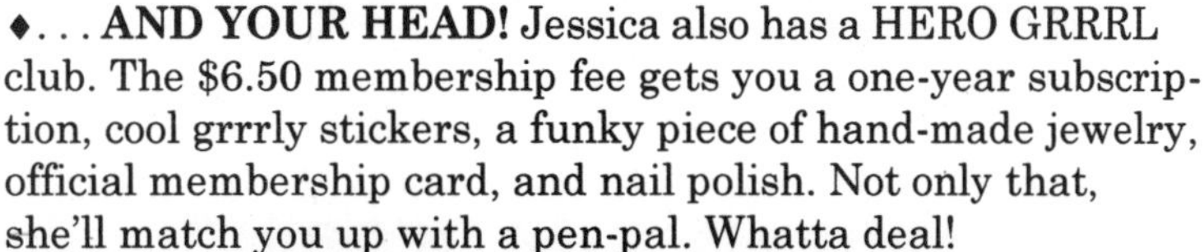

♦. . . **AND YOUR HEAD!** Jessica also has a HERO GRRRL club. The $6.50 membership fee gets you a one-year subscription, cool grrrly stickers, a funky piece of hand-made jewelry, official membership card, and nail polish. Not only that, she'll match you up with a pen-pal. Whatta deal!

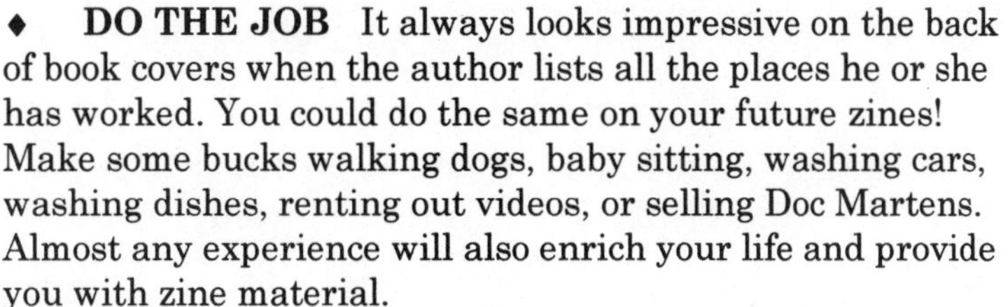

♦ **DO THE JOB** It always looks impressive on the back of book covers when the author lists all the places he or she has worked. You could do the same on your future zines! Make some bucks walking dogs, baby sitting, washing cars, washing dishes, renting out videos, or selling Doc Martens. Almost any experience will also enrich your life and provide you with zine material.

This is what the savviest zine-heads say about how they pay for their creations:

Christine Merriman, DESTROY THE EVIDENCE: "I don't buy anything else until [my zine] is printed."

Thomas, ONE QUIET VOICE: "If I have no money saved up, I just get a job for a couple of weeks to pay for it."

Jeff Guarino, THE RUMBLING UNDERNEATH: "Hard-working wife."

Gretchen Christina Lowther, GOOD FAERIE: "If I had any sense, I'd see that there's no way I can afford it."

After you've made enough money for your first run of zines, you'll need to keep it up. But at least now you have a product with which to entice your audience. The charms of your soul-child should be able to lure readers from all corners of the cosmos, or at least the coffee houses.

Of course, other factors will help as well. For instance, don't price yourself out of the market. In the beginning it's a good idea not to make your zine so phat-and-glam that you'll have to charge more than about a dollar and a stamp for it. Change can be a hassle in the mail, and more than one bill might put off your buyer until they've actually thrilled to the taste of your concoction. Plus, the more money you charge, the more your readers will be tempted to write a check. (Try explaining to your bank teller why s/he should cash something made out to THROBBING KNUCKLES!) The possibility of losing a buck or two in the mail shouldn't dissuade someone from sending cash. But don't undercharge. Figure out your costs, then price your zine so you'll at least break even.

You will probably end up giving away a lot of free copies. Friends may ask to see your zine and even the most well-intentioned might not think about giving you that buck. Try to let them know that if they want more of that dazzling prose rainbow and potent image whirlwind, they'll need to pay up.

Some zinesters avoid the whole money hassle by asking for a trade (another zine, old postcard, 7" record, etc.) Unfortunately, you'll still have to find some bucks for the basics.

Since now you have a product, why not try setting up something similar to that lemonade stand gig you had going as a kid? And this time don't forget to put the sugar in!

SPEAK UP

SPREAD THE WORD

We think the most effective way to get your zine seen is WOM. No, WOM is not a guide to zines. It is just a way others can hear about you: WORD OF MOUTH.

When someone's way into a zine, they'll most likely be inclined to check out every other zine that's recommended in it. It's kind of like love. (Admit it—you'll usually try to read every book and see every movie the object of your affection mentions). So make yourself known to other zinesters. This could mean sending out some free copies. A loving, deeply felt word of praise from someone who really gets it will do more for rocketing your zine out there than almost anything else. And remember to reciprocate. When you fall in love with a zine, hype it.

DISTRO FEVER

Distribution can be as creative as any other aspect of zine-ing. Here's CATBOX ROOM's Lisa Maslowe's interpretation of our bout with Distro Fever . . .

1.) PUBS: If you ask most zinemaniacs about how to get their zine seen, they will probably mention their bible, *Factsheet Five*. Well we have already written enough love sonnets to *F5*. But let's just say, if your zine is in it, or *Maximum Rock 'n' Roll*, or *Zine World*, or any of the publications devoted to zine reviews, you'll have a great chance of finding new readers. Also, don't dismiss the smaller DIYdistros.

2.) **STORES**: You can pound, sk8, or rock the pavement to record stores, boutiques, tattoo parlors, mag stands, etc. and ask if the owners will carry your baby on consignment (make sure they pay up for the copies they sell.) Stores might also want to carry your back issues, so remember: hold onto all your originals no matter how old they are. Many zinesters take their creations with them when they travel and hit stores in other cities as well.

3.) **MAILING LIST**: Start compiling a list using all your friends' and acquaintances' addresses, then ask them for their friends' lists, too. Swap. At shows or parties, distribute free copies and ask people to give you their addresses. Once you've got a list, you can do a mailing to announce new issues or possibly get subscribers who'll pay you a certain amount a year to have all issues sent to them. Caution: One zinester lost her mailing and subscriber list on her computer. Be sure you have a hard copy and back up on a disk!

4.) **SCHOOL:** What better place to distribute? You have a ready-made captive audience who *needs* your zine to help brighten the classroom gloom with humor, poetic angst, slamming rants, magic comic galaxies, and other wonders. Maybe you have an exceptionally cool English teacher who will encourage you to work on your zine and even accept it as a writing project like one of Stephanie HOSPITAL GOWN's teachers did. But when Stephanie realized she had to tone things down, she stopped giving out her zine at school and found other readers. Some girls at a private school in L.A. got suspended for distributing their controversial zine on campus, so watch out!

5.) **WORK:** Not only can your job serve as the source of an entire zine like FAST FOOD JANITOR, GULP LIFE (about working at a 7-11), and TEMP SLAVE, but it can also be a good place to find readers.

No matter how busy you get, don't rip people off. Send them the zine they ordered, and try to do it as soon as possible. Use some zinettiquette!

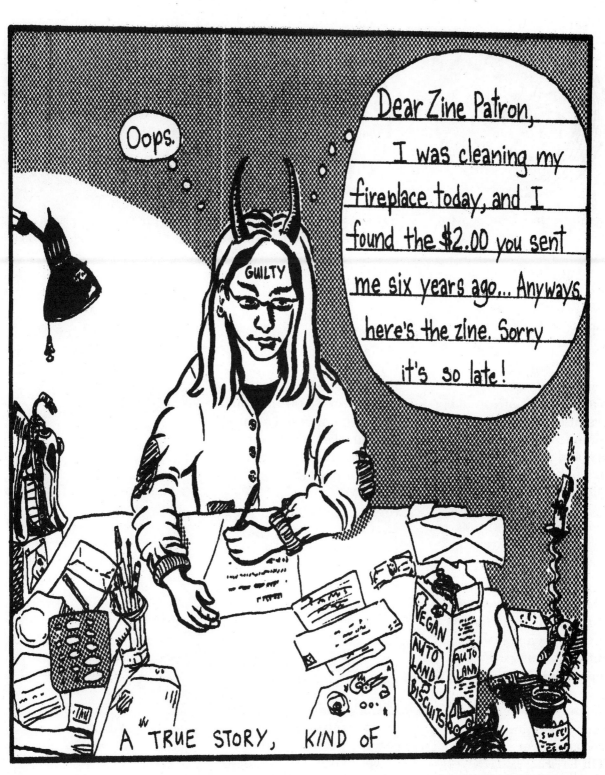

Illustrations by Lisa Maslowe

SURF'S UP

THE INTERNET AND E-ZINES

Perhaps the term "surfing the Net" was created because the possibilities on the Internet are as vast and endless as that deep, swirly, power-packed ocean.

If you have managed to stay underwater about online computer usage, either due to a lack of resources and information, or in rebellion—committed to simplicity, purity, and all things non-technical—here's some info to help you decide whether or not to dive into the world of e-zines. (The **e** stands for electronic, if you were in the dark!)

To get online, you'll need access to a computer, a modem, and a phone line. Then you'll have to choose an ISP (Internet Service Provider). For more info on all of this, you could check out any of the countless books that'll guide you online. A couple of good choices are INTERNET FOR KIDS: A BEGINNER'S GUIDE TO SURFING THE NET by Ted Pedersen and Francis Moss (no matter how old you are, it's basic and easy to read) and NET CHICK, by super cybergrrl Carla Sinclair.

If you don't have the necessary stuff, there are plenty of places popping up that offer online usage: Coffee houses (which charge in the vicinity of $5.00 an hour), schools (at most universities, you can even have your own email address), and community centers throughout the country.

What does all this have to do with zines? Well, on the Internet, there is a whole world of e-zines that just keeps getting bigger every day. As with most things, there are pros and cons to e-zines.

Let's start with the good news:

1. Gotta read a zine **NOW**? Don't want to take the time to write a letter, stuff an envelope, buy a stamp, wait for a reply? Or you don't want to bother going to the one store in town that sells zines and only carries issues you've already read? Just hop on your keyboard and get surfin'. You can access e-zines immediately.

2. Except for what you're already coughing up to be online, **E-ZINES ARE FREE!**

3. Most Web sites have *links* which, with just a click of your mouse, can lead you to more and more e-zines.

4. There's usually a place to communicate directly with the zinester, either by clicking on a certain spot or writing to a listed email address.

5. Some people can write more freely on a computer than on paper—maybe because it seems less permanent. A computer can also give a stronger sense of anonymity. And you don't need a P.O.box.

6. E-zines can include SOUNDS and MOVING IMAGES!

Illustrations by Brian Ralph, FIREBALL

Sounds incredibly enticing? How could there be anything wrong with all this? Well...

1. Many people don't feel comfortable totally exposing themselves online. There is absolutely no way to control just who's going to read your gut-wrenching, soul-pouring sharings. As much as we want to believe that most people are basically good and respectful, there are always exceptions. Hillary has a web site for her book GIRL POWER (**http://www.girlpower.com**). The site is there to encourage creative self-expression as a means to empowerment, and there are several places where people can contribute their most personal writing. Unfortunately, the disrespectful behavior of a few visitors has discouraged others from being so revealing.

2. Unless something is designed *spectacularly*, we find a lot of e-zines are hard to read. Often, you spend a lot more time clicking and waiting for the next area to download, than you do actually reading the e-zines.

* * *

You've probably noticed that the focus of this chapter so far is about you as *reader* of

e-zines. How about you as *writer?* There are basically two kinds of e-zines: those accessed by email or by a Universal Resource Locator (URL) which is a Website address. To do a zine by email, simply type and mail. When it comes to designing your own zine Web site, graphics and all, you can learn how to do this by reading specific books on the subject, as well as checking out software programs.

The Internet is also a brilliant place to promote your printed zine. There are some home pages/Web sites that give you ordering information, as well as bulletin boards where you can find and post info.

Countless zinesters rave about one particular way to spread the word: Online mailing lists. When you subscribe to mailing lists, you automatically get all the email that's posted on the lists by the other subscribers. These are a great way of creating a network of support and friendship, and of sharing information about your printed zines with like-minded people.

There are also newsgroups available on Usenet, some created by good ol' *F5*. These are places where aspiring, curious or old-hat zinesters can discuss, what else, ZINES!

You can look for collaborators, plug your creation, read reviews of zines, dish distributors, etc. (**alt.zines;alt.ezines; alt.binaries.zines**).

Speaking of *F5*, of course it would pop up on the Internet as well! Not only does their site include the reviews that appear in the printed gem, but also *links* to: all reviewed e-zines, archives of over 1,000 e-zines, and places to find printed zines (catalogs, books, etc.) as well as other zine sources. It even has essays and articles. Check **it out!** (**http://www. well.com/ conf/f5/ f5index2.html**).

To access countless e-zines, one can use a Search Engine (**AltaVista, Yahoo, Lycos, Excite, etc.**) Searching for e-zines on America Online's web browser alone, brought up 5,229 matches. *Just one* of those is John Labovitz's e-zine site which then gives over 1,500 listings. A search on AltaVista brings up 60,000 possible responses. When you click on each of those, you'll be led to more. The possibilities are endless.

You're bound to trip on something you love—from a DIY skateboard to a band of celestial adolescents . . .

STEP 1

Aw, why the long face?
You can make a skate-board out of an old roller skate.

STEP 2

You'll need:

1. an old roller skate
2. a piece of wood
3. a drill or grinder
4. a saw
5. a wrench
6. a flathead screwdriver
7. nuts and bolts
8. riser pads
9. a bearing lubricant
10. a sharpened pencil

STEP 3

With your sharpened pencil, sketch your shape onto your piece of wood. Then take your saw and cut the shape out of the wood. Use sandpaper to finish off any rough edges. Paint, polyurethane, or stain wood to seal and protect it.

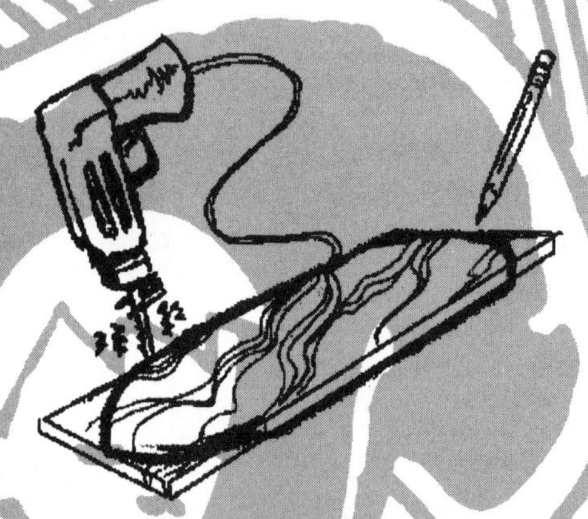

STEP 4

Take your old roller skate and turn it upside down. If you have vise, use it to keep the skate steady. Use the flathead screwdriver to take the trucks apart. You may have to use a wrench to loosen the lock nut under the bushings (the rubber thing) if the bolt won't turn with the screwdriver. The hanger should now be off the truck and you should be able to see clearly the three or four rivets that hold the base plate to the skate; take your drill or grinder and remove the heads of the rivets. When you have completely mutilated the heads of the rivets, the base plate should come off easily.

http://www.charged.com/tar/stories/oldboard/step1.htm

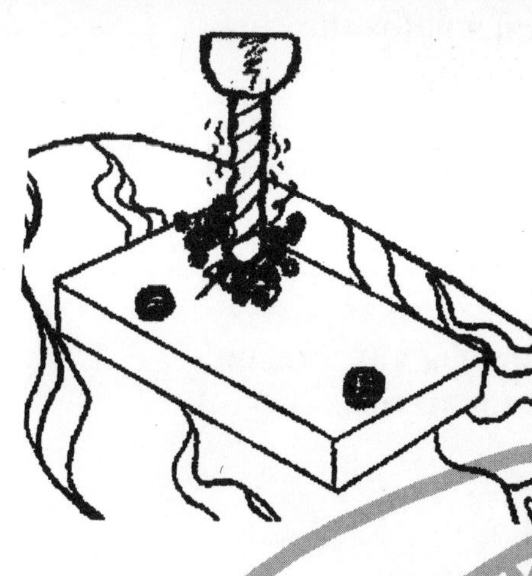

STEP 5

Cut risers for the trucks to sit on; these can be made out of wood, but rubber or plastic provide extra shock absorption. Mark the hole pattern of the base plate onto your risers. Determine where the center of your board is, then place the risers where you will want the trucks to be. Drill the mounting holes through the risers and the deck at the same time to assure proper alignment. Make sure the middle of the trucks falls in the middle of the board.

STEP 6

Bolt the base plates to the risers and the deck. You may have to enlarge the holes on the baseplate if you are going to use standard size skateboard hardware. Reassemble the trucks. Adjust the trucks by tightening the screw down into the baseplate. When the trucks are just right, lock them in place with the nut under the bushings. By locking down the nut, you can make the trucks as loose as you want without any fear of them coming apart. Add grip tape to taste. Racing stripes are always in style. Clean and lubricate the bearings thoroughly before you ride.

STEP 7

Skate and enjoy!

BONUS: SkateBoard 2000

Welcome to

Hey, what is this?

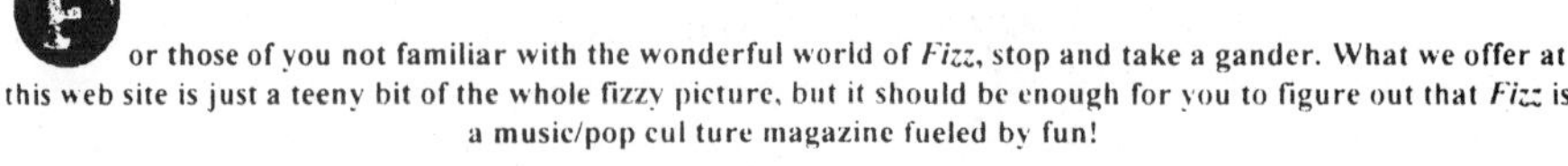

For those of you not familiar with the wonderful world of *Fizz*, stop and take a gander. What we offer at this web site is just a teeny bit of the whole fizzy picture, but it should be enough for you to figure out that *Fizz* is a music/pop cul ture magazine fueled by fun!

So what are you waiting for? Get rolling through Fizzyspace now! (Here's where we should probably put a disclaimer because we have no idea what the laws of the net are--*Fizz* is not for young kids!

Tune in, Wig out, *Fizz* on!
And let the fizziness begin!

VIVIEN'S VIBES:
Teen Angels!

by Vivien Dunn

(l-r: Julie, Lisa & Kelly with Vivien in front!)

When I interviewed the Teen Angels, it was really cool because I was having my slumber party because it was my birthday party on October 10. But since you can't have slumber parties during the week, we had to have it on the weekend. When we were doing the interview, it was just a coincidence that I was also having my party on the same day. I had all of my best friends at my slumber party, like Rebecca who also lived in Los Angeles, but I didn't know there. She was the very first kid I met here in Seattle. Leta, my best friend from Magnolia, was there too. I knew her because we met in a little park near a house and her mom introduced me to her. My friend, Rose, that my step-mother caught walking to her house, because she lives on almost the exact same street as I do in Queen Anne. And Jasmine, my best friend from school, who I sometimes walk home with when I don't have to go to the library.

The interview was really cool because when they came me and my friends were painting stuff on ourselves. And Kelly painted a little tattoo on my shoulder which we was really funny because I had to keep my shirt up over my shoulder. And my friend, Jasmine, was asking questions. She would ask questions and I would have to say, "OK, Jasmine, it's my turn to be asking the questions here." And it was really funny because two of my friends--Leta and Rose--were kind of embarrassed and they didn't ask any questions. It was really funny.

During the interview, they gave me a really cool t-shirt that says Teen Angel and has a star on either side of it. And it's *really* cool because it's my favorite color, purple! Then after the interview, we all had pizza which is really good. We had pineapple and bacon and plain ol' pineapple. And we had one with peppers on it and one with cheese. And since I was doing the interview, I got really hungry and so I took two pieces of it. And one of my friends said, "Do you think that's enough for you?" And I said, "No.Ó

And after that, we had a polar pizza that I'd been wanting to try for a long time. It had caramel and chocolate and I think a chocolate chip crust. And it was really good. Then after that I opened the presents. I got a vampire book that has a whole bunch of different stories, and I got a mood necklace that has the mood in a star. And I got two lipsticks, one's dark pink and one's light pink, but Cathy won't let me wear either of them. I also got this fake plastic hand with a $10 bill in it. And I got a Gak thing where you just push the Gak out, and there's little creatures there, and it's really weird.

I thought the band was really cool and they were all really pretty. They were really fun to be with. I hope one day they play at a little place where I can go, because I'm not yet 21. Actually I won't be 21 for a long time, and I'd like to see them before nine years come.

Vivien: Why do you call yourselves Teen Angels?
Kelly: Because it was the only name we could think of.
Vivien: Are you teens or angels?
(laughter)
Julie: They're teens, and I'm an angel.
Kelly: I'm both. *(pointing to Kim)* Teen. *(pointing to Julie)* Angel. *(pointing to self)* Both!
Vivien: Why are there no boys in your band?
Julie: No boys allowed.
Kelly: They have cooties. You know that! How come there are no boys at your party?
Vivien: It's a slumber party. They [the evil parents] wouldn't allow me to.
Kelly: See, my mom wouldn't allow me to have boys in the band.
Vivien: Believe me, there's a couple of boys I would've invited.
Julie: Oh, really? Whoo!
(laughter)
Vivien: How old are you?
Julie: Fifteen.
Kelly: Oh, great! Sixteen.
Lisa: Nineteen.
Kelly: I just got my driver's license.
Lisa: Really?
Julie: Go on to the next question!
Vivien: What kind of posters do you like?
Julie: Lindsey Kuhn [Austin silk-screen poster artist] posters!
Kelly: Good one! That artwork's going to be pretty nice now! ... You know, big posters of boys. Scott Baio, John Travolta ...
Jasmine: *(whispering to Viv)* Can I ask them a question?
Vivien: OK.
Jasmine: Have you guys seen *Pulp Fiction*?

http://www.io.com/~fizz/

Excerpt from piece by Vivien Dunn

LISTEN UP

ADVICE

The best overall advice we can give to our readers about zine-ing is this: Don't be a zine-o-phobe. Go for it. And listen to what the experts have to say:

Nicole Seymour, ODD GRRL OUT: "Don't let anyone say u suck or put down your work! Do it yourself and don't change any of your opinions for other people!"

Abraham Katzman, FLAMING JEWBOY and I'M OVER BEING DEAD: "Simultaneously embrace and explode cliché."

Mariah McDougall, MAGDALENE and REWM: ". . . it's bound to change someone's life if it comes from your heart instead of yer nagging little jimeny cricket of self-censorship . . .let 'er rip . . .you have to scream real loud if anybody is gonna hear you . . . and believe me, there are plenty of ways to scream even if you're whispering . . . (you) are contributing to the revolution just by allowing these things to slip onto paper and be widely distributed to the world . . ."

Lorena Melgoza, UGLY: "Always sign your work—even if it's an alias. Always sign it so that it is yours and no one else can take credit for it."

Thomas Christian, CHRONICLES OF DISORDER: "Don't think too much—i.e. paralysis byanalysis."

Gretchen Christina Lowther, GOOD FAERIE: "advice for aspiring and most definitely future zine stars: i know handfuls of people who just talk about making a zine. you don't get to it that way at all — get to it which means write even if it's crap, don't even hesitate. maybe it ends up not taking, but when you start you can't think too much about it. and eventually it's inside you. it's easy to do — you have stories to tell."

Andrea H., SCREAMING MIMI: "READ ZINES. read lots and lots of zines and find out what you like to read . . ."

Christine Merriman, DESTROY THE EVIDENCE: "it sounds ridiculous, but . . . complete a first issue, critique it, then destroy it the next morning and recreate."

Rob Northrup, DELINQUENT WENCH and PUNK PALS UNWASHED: "Zines are for exploring, so don't listen to anyone's 'advice!' INCLUDING THIS!"

OUTRO

Tania Rudy has made friends all over the world through STOOL PIGEON. Ceci received a letter from the actress Heather Mattarrazo after raving about her film *Welcome to the Dollhouse* in SUBURBIA. Al Hoff had a book published based on her zine THRIFT SCORE. Stephanie Kuhnert heard from girls who had been sexually abused and were helped by reading HOSPITAL GOWN.

By now, it's obvious: We think you should have zine mania! We've expounded on the joys of a full mailbox, new pals, and shared revelations about everything from thrift scores to love scars. But if all this isn't enough for you—if saying something the way only you can, in an open forum, and becoming part of a subculture as varied and colorful as any that exists, doesn't quite do it—we'd like you to hear what some other zinesters get from doing their zines, and why they're hooked:

Gretchen Christina Lowther, GOOD FAERIE: "I write as a reason to live."

Michelle Morgan Cross, ADVERSARIA and SMUDGE: "I get inspiring bursts of gleesome satisfaction, sporadic wallops of ziney-zeal and, frequently, the incentive I need to persevere through the wretched stumble that teen life often seems to be. Yup, that about sums it up."

Erin McCarley, GLAMOUR QUEEN: "... sometimes i'll feel really depressed while working on a zine and afterwards when it's done i'll go back and read it and see how honest, and yes, depressing it was, but also how much hope underlies in the writings, and strength and it's so awesome to be able to re-validate yourself over and over again. to be able to sit and KNOW, even when things are sucking really bad that YEAH I CAN COUNT ON MYSELF."

Thomas, ONE QUIET VOICE: "My zine allows me to be me to strangers. I normally would want to curl up into a ball or go slink off somewhere when I'm around people I don't know, but this allows me to show people who I am at the same time I'm throwing up my shields . . ."

Gina, PRIVATE CATHOLIC: "I get the satisfaction of knowing that I have created something—without adults helping me or corporations backing me. I have made something myself, that is completely me—uncensored and of my own creation."

Melissa Albach, LOOKING GLASS GIRL ZINE: "People die spiritually from keeping their truth inside. I felt that way for so long because I was afraid to say my truth . . ."

Lisa, BITCH DYKE WHORE: "My zine has helped me sort out my emotions, especially about getting raped. I went to a shrink for a while and it never helped, but after I started my zine I felt a million times better . . . my zine gives me the opportunity to scream it out to the world, because i'm not going to be silent anymore."

Michael, CULTURE FREAK: "Kicks man, kicks."

Thomas Christian, CHRONICLES OF DISORDER: "I get small rectangular shaped lesions under pads of fingertips from excessive staplings."

There's really only one reason to zine—not because we think you should, not because you might get a book deal or new friends, but because you have to do it *for you*. We hope this book has given you some inspiration, the way our encounters with zinemaniacs have inspired us.

Just imagine the words your heart would use if it could talk. Would it rant and scream? Whisper and giggle? What pictures are in your head? Collages of gargoyles and angels? Drawings of skeletons and swirling lovers? What would your soul feel like if you could put a stamp on it and drop it in the mail?

Maybe the answer lies in the zine that only your heart, mind and soul can create.

"it's like i'm making myself tangible. so i stop feeling like this sordid sad little waif in the wind :) it's what i fill my boots up with every morning, what i use to call my father up and tell him goodbye forever, what i throw around when i need some space and what i put on the plate when i'm telling my secrets . . . i let it out in a breath and drown myself in it in my mind . . . it's all the things i have to say to survive. i could live on words. i could exist on breath alone . . . it's a miracle i'm still standing after the stampede of demons i've been letting out lately . . . but i'm right here. alive, laughing out some rage and crying out some joy. it's amazing to be real . . . so this is what all the fuss is about."

Mariah McDougall, MAGDELENE and REWN

RESOURCES

From the time we started compiling zines and writing ZINE SCENE, to the time it actually gets into your hot little hands, several years will have passed and, from our experience, addresses change much more quickly than that.

We don't want you to be frustrated when you order zines from an out-of-date address and don't get a response. So what we will do is provide information on how to find some of the larger publications that list *currently* published zines.

These publications not only have zinesters contact addresses, but they also include lists of distros and zine-friendly bookstores.

FACTSHEET FIVE

P.O. Box 170099

San Francisco, CA 94117-0099

MAXIMUM ROCK 'N' ROLL

P.O. Box 460760

San Francisco, CA 94146-0760

ZINE WORLD

924 Valencia St. #203

San Francisco, CA 94110

Keep an eye out for these other small distros and bookstores zinesters have mentioned:

DISTROS: Riot Grrrl Press, Bratgirl, Kid Revolution, Pander, Power Toot Media Empire, The Way Sassy, Schmegma Gumbo, Reading Frenzy, Veronica, For the Cause, Punk Planet, Pro-Negative, Pez Action/ Lame Ass, Heroes for Today and Million Year Picnic.

BOOKSTORES: See Hear (New York, NY), Quimby's (Chicago, IL), Atomic Books (Baltimore, MD), Reading Frenzy (Portland, OR).

AUTHORS' BIOS

TEN COOL THINGS ABOUT FRANCESCA LIA BLOCK

by Hillary Carlip

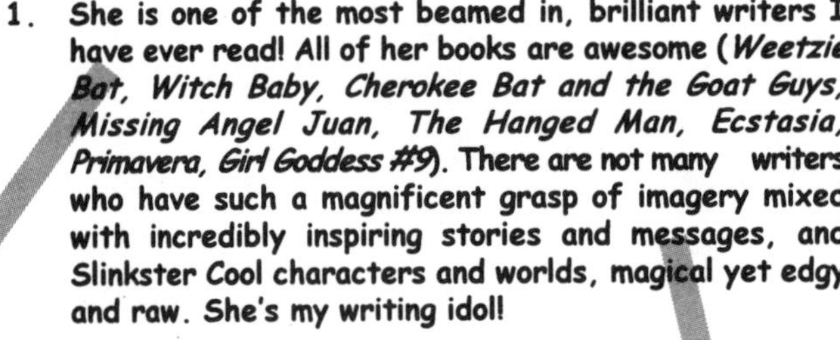

1. She is one of the most beamed in, brilliant writers I have ever read! All of her books are awesome (*Weetzie Bat, Witch Baby, Cherokee Bat and the Goat Guys, Missing Angel Juan, The Hanged Man, Ecstasia, Primavera, Girl Goddess #9*). There are not many writers who have such a magnificent grasp of imagery mixed with incredibly inspiring stories and messages, and Slinkster Cool characters and worlds, magical yet edgy and raw. She's my writing idol!

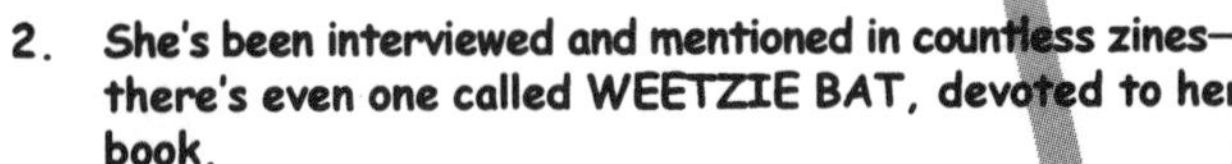

2. She's been interviewed and mentioned in countless zines—there's even one called WEETZIE BAT, devoted to her book.

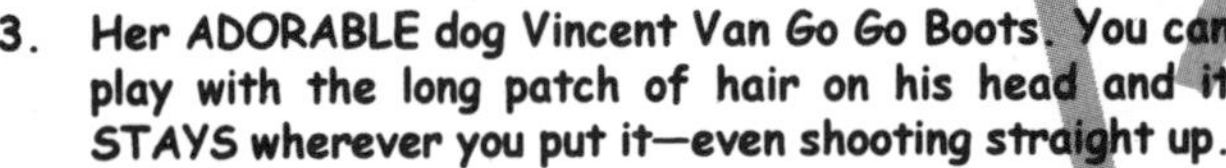

3. Her ADORABLE dog Vincent Van Go Go Boots. You can play with the long patch of hair on his head and it STAYS wherever you put it—even shooting straight up.
4. She eats as oddly as I do. Non-dairy brown-rice-sweet butterscotch pudding, a shared fave!
5. She was punk WAAAY back when, slamming at clubs in L.A. with her constantly changing hair color.
6. She loves faeries—BOTH KINDS!
7. She comes from an incredible family of artists and poets.
8. She really cares about contributing to others, giving all she can, moving and inspiring and educating.
9. She's an amazing dancer. From ballet to . . . well, let's just say I've seen her go CRAAAZY on the dance floor.
10. When she's inspired, WATCH OUT! She's written incredible screenplays in a week, books in not much longer than that.